Reflected

Residencies

EDITOR
Irmeli Kokko

CONTRIBUTORS
dylan ray arnold
Francesca Bertolotti-Bailey
Océane Bruel
Pau Català
Taru Elfving
Kalle Hamm
Maria Hirvi-Ijäs
Miina Hujala
Leena Kela
Anna Kirveennummi
Irmeli Kokko
Anders Kreuger
Miriam La Rosa
Vytautas Michelkevičius
Katia Porro

COPY EDITING AND PROOFREADING
Anders Kreuger

GRAPHIC DESIGN
Marina Veziko

PRINTING AND BINDING
Tallinna Raamatutrükikoda
Tallinn, Estonia

FIRST EDITION
2024

PUBLISHED BY
Mousse Publishing in collaboration
with Kone Foundation/Saari Residence
Mynämäki, Finland

DISTRIBUTED BY
Mousse Publishing
Contrappunto s.r.l.
Via Pier Candido Decembrio 28
20137 Milan, Italy

AVAILABLE THROUGH
Mousse Publishing, Milan
moussemagazine.it

ISBN 9788867496310

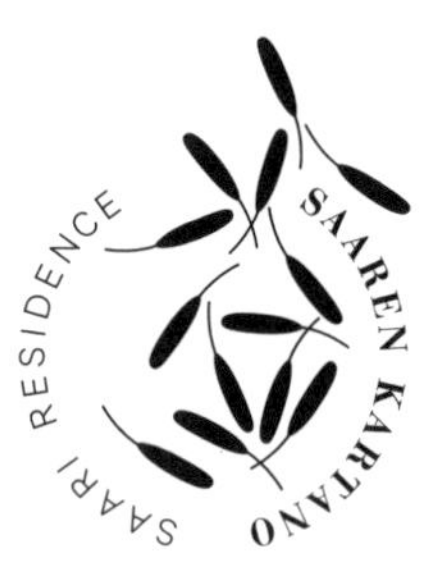

Mousse
Publishing

Residencies Reflected

Edited by Irmeli Kokko

Index

Foreword

Irmeli Kokko

2023 was an exceptional year, because it saw the appearance of three significant books examining artist residencies and mobility for artists. *On Care: A Journey into the Relational Nature of Artists' Residencies*, edited by Pawel Mendrek, Elke aus dem Moore, Ika Sienkiewicz-Nowacka, Bojana Panevska, Denise Helene Sumi and Ewa Zasada[1], presents new research on the relational nature of the relationships that emerge within the time limits set by artist residencies. The focus is on the dialogue between the artists and the institution and on the working and living environment in artist residencies, in this case mainly in Central and Eastern Europe.

Ukhona Ntsali Mlandu's e-publication *An invitation to transform your vision of the cultural mobility ethic from an African perspective*[2], published by the Brussels-based platform On the Move, is a profound essay and invitation to change our thoughts and assumptions about the mobility patterns, seen from the reality of the African context. *Bringing Worlds Together*, finally, an anthology by writers including the celebrated artists Howardina Pindell and Mierle Laderman Ukeles, was edited by Kari Conte and Susan Hapgoord[3] for the New York-based Rethinking Residencies network. It examines residencies as particular sites of visual art production marked by close interaction between artists, communities, and the environment.

The collection of essays *Contemporary Artist Residencies: Reclaiming Time and Space*, edited by Taru Elfving, Pascal Gielen and myself and published in 2018[4], was one of the most extensive anthologies examining the development trends of artist residencies in the creative economy.

Those recent publications are now joined by *Residencies Reflected*. It has developed out of a symposium with invited researchers and writers at the Saari Residence in Mynämäki, Finland, in August 2021, for which I was the curator.[6] The symposium had no theme, apart from being a gathering of specialists and practitioners from the field of artist residencies and a free forum for discussing, presenting new research and forging new connections. The Saari Residence, which is part of the Kone Foundation, commissioned this book as a continuation of its long-term support for different aspects of residency activities and asked me to edit it.

This publication consists of nine essays and two artist contributions, and one interview. The contributors are residency professionals working globally and locally, researchers, curators and artists. The methods vary from artistic to academic research and they represent a variety of approaches to residencies, from investigations of alternative histories and geographies to deliberations on possible and probable futures and from reflections on artistic freedom to close readings of individual artworks.

The contributions, dating from between 2021 and 2023, are born from the pandemic and reflect experiences and observations unlocked by that unprecedented and unpredictable state of global affairs. When the lockdowns happened, a whole world used to the self-evidence of mobility was upended. The process of globalisation with its limitless space-time and open-ended possibilities suddenly ground to a halt. In its place came uncertainty and fear, which were both exacerbated by Russia's invasion of Ukraine in February 2022.

In our part of the world the war has brought new hard borders. As I write this, Alexei Navalny has been murdered in his prison in the Siberian Arctic. Plato's *Symposium* has appeared on a list of books to be removed from bookstores in Saint Petersburg. Finland has joined NATO and temporarily closed its 1,289 kilometres long eastern border to prevent illicit crossings. Elsewhere this new state of ongoing war may lead to the dismantling of borders. It is unclear what kind of world we will be living in when our book is published later this spring.

While residencies have traditionally provided time and space for free artistic work, research and experiments anywhere in the world, they now also imply an awareness of and relationship with the environment. The ecological crisis has affected the processes and methods for making art and its verbalisation as an activity and a mode of thinking. For the individual resident, the residency experience often becomes a conscious interaction with the living or non-living creatures of the immediate environment.

For artist residency organisations, the ecological crisis has created a need to adopt new practices, guidelines and regulations. Its effects extend to the ways of supporting artistic work, the duration of residency periods and the commitment to place. Artistic and scientific inquisitiveness are coming together in programmatic ways. The current vocabulary of artist residencies includes ecological and cultural sustainability, refuge (or safe space), care, virtuality and slow travel.

How are artist residencies and their key concepts – time, space, place, community, mobility – activated to reflect current reality? What kind of sustainability do we need? What kind of security can residences offer artists? Can art be both a refuge and a tool for sustainable development? A big challenge of artist residencies today is how to redefine the role and practices of residencies in such a way that they can meet new challenges in times of uncertainty (Dr. Vytautas Michelkevičius's essay).

By facilitating encounters and connections, artist residencies generate knowledge about places, environments and communities, but also about the consequences of cultural collisions. The isolation during the pandemic meant not only a standstill but gave rise also to new observations and ideas about artist residencies and their practices. The futurist Anna Kirveennummi emphasises the growing importance of experimentation in art and science. 'With the means of art and science, we can push boundaries and employ a holistic, experimental approach that integrates multiple perspectives [...] How could these alternative practices spread the idea of hope-building and the importance of speculative dreaming?' (interview with Leena Kela and Dr. Anna Kirveennummi).

The globalising utopias of the 1990s emphasised border-crossings between cultures and limitless mobility, networking and interaction. Being too attached to the local was seen as a transgression or as resistance against the forces of the global. 'The global village' looked utopian from the perspective of Western urban centres.[2] Today the interpretation of the poetics of mobility as a historically Western phenomenon is being challenged and complemented by a fairer historical account of how artists and other thinkers moved about freely in other parts of the world (Dr. Pau Catà's essay). By their nature, artist residencies strive to overcome distances and differences. Their potential is to connect different kinds of people. Sustainable cultural diplomacy and cultural policy must therefore understand artist residencies as social actors (Dr. Maria Hirvi-Ijäs's essay).

Residencies can produce new knowledge by modelling ecologically sustainable lifestyles. Renewable residency practice could mean, for example, a firmer commitment to developing more ecological daily routines, and at the same time more utopian social thought, than was required within a residency culture based on rapid global mobility and short duration. The importance of a residency would be its relative focus on alternative and experimental lifestyles as part of the cultural ecosystem (Francesca Bertolotti-Bailey's essay).

This attitude represents a continuation of the European, and particularly Eastern European, tradition of artist colonies. What many of those had in common was a critical attitude towards the harm to society and the environment caused by the industrial revolution and by urbanisation. At the same time artist colonies embodied aspirations for alternative communal lifestyles. Striving towards a new kind of community of artists and craftsmen, many of them aimed at social reforms influenced by socialist ideals. Alternative ways of life were tried out, such as Tolstoyism or the idea of free love. It was essential that the colonies were based on social networks, the environment and the place as a whole rather than on the presence of charismatic individual artists.[7]

During the pandemic many residencies adapted their working methods by introducing virtual residencies. Is a virtual community a 'real art residency', a place for making and sharing art? What kind of new observations and ideas are possible in the virtual encounters and how are they related to recent art history? (Dr. Miriam La Rosa's essay). The anthropologist Victor Turner studied rituals and found that they, especially when aiming at solving problems, are social processes of a performative nature.[8] Does travel as ritual become a performative part of the residency? Slow travelling has been adopted as an ecologically sustainable form of moving from one place to another. Can it be a way to investigate pre-existing mode of transit as new opportunities for artistic research, in the form of a mobile residency? (Miina Hujala's essay).

In the current conditions of ecological crisis the process of making art is total – as total as our experience of the pandemic. When our relationship with nature and the environment changes, our bodily sensations and experiences also change and become strained reflections of our sensations and feelings (or affects). Moreover, materiality can be the fundamental motivation for artistic activity, whether it replaces ideologies or coexists with them. The starting point of a residency or an artistic process activity can be a fixation exclusively with the environment, with buildings, materials, the soil, the flora and fauna (Taru Elfving's essay). Resident artists may work directly with animate and inanimate nature, in which they and other humans become fellow travellers, participants or even just 'matter that flows through a building and attaches itself to them at different times'.[9]

Ecologically and culturally sustainable residency activity also requires attention to the diversity and freedom of art. The most important players in artist residencies are the artists who work in them. They give birth to new art, new methods of practicing art, new ethics and aesthetics (Anders Kreuger's essay).

How we exist in the world as relational, physical, psychological and neurological beings is articulated in works of art and philosophy. A work of art is a multifaceted entity consisting of visible or invisible ideas, materials, experiences and modes of reception. Yet in the context of artist residencies the artwork is not the main focus. The residency is regarded as a unit of time, a process of artistic research in which the site of the residency, the making of the work and its presentation may be separated by considerable distances. The residence as a lived experience or environment is usually not presented in an articulated manner in the presentation phase, in the context of exhibitions. Instead, the symbolic value of artist residencies is formed by the structure it offers for the individual creative process. They are a part of the art world that often remains invisible to the public.

One of the intentions behind the book is to articulate how time and place can be turned into artistic method and how residencies may encourage ethically and ecologically sustainable thinking and practice, which then become manifest in works of art. I have therefore invited three artists to author two artworks as autonomous contributions to the book, in an attempt to lend more visibility to their practices. My choice of artists was influenced by the significant role that residencies as institutions have played in the development of their creative processes, methods and ecological mindset.

Kalle Hamm has been doing environmental and botanical research for a long time, both in the Saari Residence and during several residency periods at the Seili Island. His and Taru

Elfving's multi-year collaboration with the Archipelago Sea Research Institute has greatly influenced the perception of what a residency can be as field research.

Océane Bruel and dylan ray arnold live in Finland and work both as a duo and separately. The artists have opted for radical openness and uncertainty, and their work is marked by a poetics and politics of materiality and corporeality, of travelling, making and exposure. The simultaneous presence of different layers of sensations and sensual experiences is characteristic of their approach to artmaking (Katia Porro's essay).

In her recent book *On Freedom*, Maggie Nelson[10] discusses the significance of Ludwig Wittgenstein's words 'the meaning of a word is its use' and the awareness that the concept of freedom is used in different language games for different purposes. Freedom is a concept that needs to be taken care of. When the concept gets blurred, it needs to be talked about. For Nelson, freedom is something that must be constantly practiced. To me this is a reminder that regardless of the crises we are facing or the ethical principles we subscribe to, we mustn't forget to keep reflecting on everything we do from the perspective of freedom: individual and collective, artistic freedom and freedom of conscience and expression. This book attempts to embody the need to take care of freedom in the expending field of artist residencies, by affirming it and facilitating it but also by questioning what it means and how it relates to other existential imperatives.

I sincerely thank all who have contributed to *Residencies Reflected*, the writers and the artists and the interviewees as well as Saari Residence in Mynämäki, its publishers, and Mousse Publishing in Milan, its international distributors. My special thanks go to Anders Kreuger, who apart from contributing one of the essays has also done the copy editing, to the designer Marina Veziko and last but not least to Leena Kela, the director of Saari Residence, without whose unwavering commitment this book would never have seen the light of day.

1 Pawel Mendrek, Elke aus dem Moore, Ika Sienkiewicz-Nowacka, Bojana Panevska, Denise Helene Sumi and Ewa Zasada (eds), *On Care: A Journey into the Relational Nature of Artists' Residencies* (Vienna: Verlag für moderne Kunst, 2023).

2 Ukhona Ntsali Mlandu, *An invitation to transform your vision of the cultural mobility ethic from an African perspective.* (Brussels: On the Move, 2023). E-book available at: https://on-the-move. org/sites/default/files/library/2023-12/OTM_ transform-vision-mobility-african-perspective.pdf.

3 Kari Conte and Susan Hapgoord (eds), *Bringing Worlds Together: A Rethinking Residencies Reader* (New York: Rethinking Residencies, 2023).

4 Taru Elfving, Pascal Gielen and Irmeli Kokko (eds), *Contemporary Artist Residencies: Reclaiming Time and Space* (Amsterdam: Valiz, 2019).

5 Some practitioners and writers prefer the more inclusive term art residencies. The dual usage is reflected in this book.

6 'My Journey: Knowledge and Exchange', Saari Well assembly of residency researchers at the Saari Residence on 18–22 August 2021. Participants: Dr. Pau Catà, Kari Conte, Taru Elfving, Jaana Eskola (organiser, Saari Residence), Patricia Healy McMeans, Riitta Heinämaa, Dr. Maria Hirvi-Ijäs, Morag Iles, Leena Kela (organiser, Saari Residence), Irmeli Kokko (curator), Dr. Miriam La Rosa (online), Ki Nurmenniemi, Dr. Kathryn S. Roberts (online), Angela Serino, Rita Vargas.

7 See Marina Dmitrieva and Laima Laučkaitė-Surgailienė (eds), *Community and Utopia: Artists' Colonies in Eastern Europe, from the Fin-de-Siècle to the Socialist Period* (Vilnius: Lithuanian Cultural Research Institute, 2017).

8 See Richard Schechner, 'Victor Turner's Last Adventure', *Anthropologica* 27, no. 1–2 (1985), pp. 190–206.

9 Inna Perheentupa, Suvi Salmenniemi and Pilvi Porkola, '"Mikä tahansa on mahdollista tässä talossa". Arkipäivän utopioiden materiaalisdiskur-siivinen rakentuminen', *Tiede & Edistys* (3/2023).

10 Maggie Nelson, *On Freedom: Four Songs of Care and Constraint* (Minneapolis: Graywolf Press, 2021), p. 4.

14

Post-Utopian Communes and Sustainability Camps: Artist Residencies as Machines for Co-Living

Francesca Bertolotti-Bailey

Francesca Bertolotti-Bailey is a producer, curator and editor with a background in economics and cultural policy, based in Turin and London. Together with the designer Ab Rogers and the neuroscientist Ash Ranpura, she recently co-founded DRU+, a design research agency operating in the fields of healthcare, culture and sustainability. Until 2022 she was the CEO of Cove Park, an artist residency in rural Scotland. Previously she worked at Kettle's Yard, the modern and contemporary art gallery of the University of Cambridge, at the Liverpool Biennial, where she co-curated the 2016 and 2018 editions, at Artissima, the contemporary art fair in Turin, and at the Fondazione Pirelli Hangar Bicocca in Milan. In 2016–18 she was Associate at Large of Council, a Paris-based organisation focused on the integration of artistic, scientific and civic ways of knowing. Since 2016 she has been the co-director of the publishing, archiving and learning platform The Serving Library.

Throughout the brief history of artist residencies, the key word associated with their rapid development on both sides of the turn of the millennium has been mobility. These days the word sounds almost objectionable. In recent years the image of the cosmopolitan residency-hopping artist jetting around the globe has been gradually replaced by that of an environmentally-conscious elite precariat drawn to a well-balanced, ethically sound and sustainable lifestyle. At least this is the case in the Global North or affluent West. In European territories thankfully free from war gestures, militant actions and institutional policies that challenge or counteract the outdated glamour of mobility are now considered the vanguard of the cultural sector. This is to describe my own situated perspective, too: one that questions the value of constant movement, staking a claim against the unlimited uberisation of life.

Amid the increasingly apparent effects of ecological breakdown, such deceleration is mainly a response to the chronically urgent need for scrapping or a least reducing our use of fossil fuels, and our speedy consumption of goods and services more generally. It is also common knowledge that the Covid-19 pandemic has exacerbated socio-economic inequality and engendered new attitudes towards domesticity, labour and travel. But despite the massive carbon savings and the pious proclamations in favour of new, sustainable futures for the art world, at the end of lockdown life artists and art professionals alike were more than happy to attend to the backlog of international appointments that the pandemic had put on hold and to socially resuscitate after months of cultural isolation.

At the same time, even those supposedly progressive households of artists already used to working from home discovered how quickly the gendered balancing act of professional, domestic and invisible labour could regress to traditionally sexist defaults, especially where children were involved. The impact of the pandemic on the labour market is still vividly underway, with union negotiations, protests and strikes battling for better pay and conditions taking place across Europe, while many corporations remain suspicious of flexible working arrangements.

Despite the inevitable gradual softening of the most radical positions formed during lockdown, the long tail of discourse around these matters seems to have produced some solid habits, commitments and expectations in terms of working and living conditions, at least within the cultural sector. It seems to me that what has really remained is a deeply felt understanding of the matrix of sustainability, along with a lack of tolerance for disrespecting it. Yet the opposite is also happening. There is a backlash against and intolerance towards sustainability discourse in line with populist politics and with a sad fatigue, inertia or fatalism that is clearly paralysing younger generations.

All in all, after speaking with many colleagues and friends from the arts sector over the last year or two I have the impression that the 'new normal' is marked by a renewed awareness of the elements that make up a good life (in the sense of *buen vivir*). The entanglements of social, financial, psychological and ecological sustainability by which we should like to increasingly measure the relative success of an individual lifestyle, institution or network are now at the centre of our attention.

In January 2021, when I landed in Scotland to take on the role of CEO of the rural artist residency Cove Park, the pandemic was at its peak. Restrictions were extreme, and sensitivities heightened. For six months I was alone with my family on the large premises of a residency built to accommodate up to 20 people at any given time. Living and working in solitude on 50 acres of land overlooking a grandiose loch felt diametrically opposite to the markedly urban life I had been enjoying in Helsinki only a few weeks earlier as a three-month resident in the single-person apartment of the Saastamoinen Foundation. I mention these recent experiences – as both guest and host in quick succession – to orient this text towards a meditation on an essential characteristic of any residential retreat. Namely, the opportunity for the conditions of cohabitation to exist outside conventional contractual arrangements and for those conditions to be apt for experimentation.

In 1927 Le Corbusier spoke of the house as a 'machine to live in' to emphasise how architecture can extend human capabilities. I have borrowed and slightly amended his expression in my title for this text, because I mean to focus on the potential of artist residencies to become new machines for sustainable co-living.

In the immediate aftermath of the pandemic it became apparent that the UK-based artists applying for a residency with us at Cove Park were generally doing so not primarily to focus on a project or collaboration, but rather as a means of healing and restoring psychological balance. They needed to escape a situation at home rendered unbearable by lockdown and find refuge from financial pressures made acute by Covid-related cancellations and postponements of gigs and commissions. They also needed to replenish their social network by seeking meaningful connections with like-minded people in a protected environment. Indeed what most residents (and staff members) were trying to do at that time, whether consciously or not, was to rekindle and reset the habits, routines and methods related to their own selves, their practice and their communities, both within and outside the space of the residency.

Artist residencies are exceptional institutions within the arts sector, being the only format where private, professional and public life are totally integrated and blurred. They are controlled, protected environments – sometimes even safe spaces – where alternative behaviours and lifestyles can be developed, implemented, tested and reprogrammed. Those residencies situated at the margins, in rural or peripheral locations, have the potential to become laboratories of sustainable living, even more so now in the wake of the pandemic.

It is no coincidence that many utopian communes from the bohemian turn of the last century and the counterculture of the 1960s and 70s were set up outside cities in the United States, Europe and China. There isn't enough space here to expand on the relationship between residential retreats, artists and the natural environment. I will instead suggest in passing that current forms of art-based co-living, as well as eco-villages and other intentional communities across the world, are often relying on the countryside, whether for growing food, re-appropriating dispossessed land or connecting with non-human ecologies.

Crucially, rural or peripheral artist residencies are characterised by a mitigation or absence of a whole plethora of social and professional pressures that artists of all disciplines usually face when they spend time on a residency in a capital city. Without the constant lure of gigs, openings, dinners and studio visits, the residents of those more isolated institutions have the opportunity to concentrate undisturbed on themselves, their practice or research, or on the temporary community of the residency, and also on the various strategies and protocols that make that focus sustainable.

Artist residencies can be productively analysed as speculative, moral or ontological spaces, if we consider the ideologies at the base of their conception, development and survival. They may be speculative spaces inasmuch as they facilitate the production and circulation of critical, theoretical, artistic discourse. They may spatially embody experiments in behaviour and social interaction that more or less radically challenge the status quo and speculate on alternative futures.

Artist residencies may be moral spaces – a term borrowed from healthcare and architecture theory – inasmuch as their spatial configuration, together with their written and implicit rules, guide the individual and the collective towards specific behaviours that the institution deems good and desirable as opposed to bad and unacceptable. One could argue that all spaces are moral spaces, but the case for morality becomes more apparent when private and public life are contained within one space of cohabitation.

Residencies may also be ontological spaces – this term is borrowed from design discourse – inasmuch as they are locations of becoming and worldmaking, both at the level of the individual, for whom the time of the residency is usually transformative, and of the collective, which may use the space of the residency to generate alternative realities.

Whether their purpose is to defend the autonomy of art, promote the exchange of knowledge, facilitate networking, uphold peer support, or a combination of these, such institutions operate as totalising organisations. The spatial configuration of the built environment together with the (un)written rules of the house and host inevitably influence the behaviour of their residents. Such factors affect not only the production of art, but all aspects of life. Sleeping, eating, working, idling, playing – all are inextricably interconnected within the semi-private environment of the residency's temporary community. This is why I'm suggesting that artist residencies are also political spaces of cohabitation. They are spaces of negotiation between and among the residents, the staff, and sometimes the local community, all benefitting (or not) from the organisation's presence or programme.

Speculative, moral, ontological, political: these are some of the intertwined descriptors of the highly charged space of the artist residency when seen both from the historical vantage of utopian co-living experiments and from a future post-utopian perspective of urgent societal transition and adaptation.

In the last ten years at least, ideological drivers related to social and ecological change have become important factors in the development and sustainability of artist residencies. These include the climate, food, and racial justice, but also inclusivity, diversity, equality, access and the politics of (self-)care. A given residency may or may not facilitate the production of cultural products that address these socio-political issues, but it unequivocally allows – and sometimes advocates – for constant experimentation with the actions and interactions that embody such concerns.

Although I would prefer to avoid associating the (mental) space of the residency with a Petri dish, I use the word 'experimentation' to point to the constant feedback loop of trial and error, the recognition of evidence, results and effects that every behaviour or action within the residency inevitably generates. Upholding certain ethical guidelines or policies, for instance enacting specific morals relative to human and non-human interaction or regulating sustainable behaviours of consumption, are foundational to the transient ecosystem of artist residencies.

This is where the heterotopic exceptionalism of the artist residency lies. It resembles life while existing outside its normal flow, enabling the production and exchange of ideas and projects around urgent societal issues, certainly, but also enacting them in real time. The circuits between cause and effect, and between action and affect, are far shorter in a closed environment where, say, a dozen people live and work side by side in relative isolation for a circumscribed period of time than they would be in the ongoing complexity and unpredictability of daily life. The house rules, the institutional culture, the temporary conflicts and alliances between residents and staff: all the strategies and protocols for living and working together (and in proximity) need to be recognised, adopted and resolved quickly to foster a positive residential experience, regardless of any wider political project.

At least in Northern Europe, the current emphasis on inclusion, diversity, equality and access has corroborated and further expanded the idea of the residency as a nominally safe space where everybody is welcome and acknowledged. The consequent adjustments in funding schemes and opportunities have given way to an increasingly segmented series of 'market niches' and specialised programmes aimed at supporting under-represented artists. This, in turn, has deepened the relation between the resident and the residency. They can increasingly enjoy a kind of elective affinity, a sympathy and a connection, based on trust and recognition. Community and solidarity come with all the perks and pitfalls of any group dynamic – mutual help, control issues, mirror behaviour, radical transparency – and with a system of rewards. For all these reasons, I believe that the residency model is conducive to the development, negotiation and transformation of radical gestures directed at intersectional forms of sustainability.

To recap: in the 1990s residencies were, at least in Europe, postulated on mobility as a driver of the geopolitical soft power of the post-cold-war European project. Its international and transcultural ideals catered to the cosmopolitan artist who a decade later would be labelled a 'digital nomad'. Today, in the face of relentless eco-socio-political crises, artist residencies everywhere seem to become retreats or refuges for generations of artists who struggle to make a living within the arts sector and/or feel unrepresented, excluded or traumatised by recent and current events. At the same time, artist residencies are morphing into political spaces concerned with pioneering speculative sustainable forms of communal working and living.

Residencies today are generally practicing radical cooperation both locally and internationally, from growing food to enforcing slow travel and from hosting refugees or artists with families to experimenting with autonomous energy production. They have never been closer in spirit to the utopian communes and intentional communities of the 1960s and 70s. I wish to point out the positive legacies of visionary thinking, commitment to alternative practices, communion with the natural environment, and free experimentation with labour, kinship and property. Yet I'm also mindful of the negative connotations that are sometimes associated with such projects, such as sexism, sectarianism, seclusion, and naïve impracticality.

Large sectors of the humanities, the arts and the social sciences are tirelessly trying to imagine alternative ways to co-exist (or co-survive) on an increasingly warm, crowded and sterile planet. Thanks to their intrinsic characteristics as institutional embodiments of collective intelligence, artist residencies seem well situated to seek effective answers to such all-encompassing problems. Yet there is little acknowledgment of what I understand to be a clear link between the models developed by mid-twentieth-century utopian counterculture, and current arts-based experiments in cohabitation. The reasons likely include political coyness, an allergy to nostalgia, the desire for artist residencies to be perceived as at the service of the individual artist rather than society as a whole – and the painful recognition that those utopian models were soon co-opted by the capitalist machine.

I'm conscious of entering dangerous territory when I hint at the opportunity for artist residencies to test, refine and ideally help distribute alternative ways of living and working. Collective intelligence, a term borrowed from socio-biology and political science, is the process by which a group of people gather, share their knowledge and skills, collaborate and perhaps even compete to solve complex problems. In other words, it is a type of wisdom and knowledge growing out of a group of people working together on a particular issue, which cannot exist at the level of the individual.

To suggest that artist residencies may be considered as laboratories of collective intelligence is to also suggest the existence of a series of issues that a given institution and its residents have collectively decided to try to unpack. This is not typical of artist residencies, unless the residents are specifically engaged in shaping some facets of the institutional policies or in some kind of decision-making workshop. On the contrary, individual freedom, time and space are generally considered the basic principles of any successful residency. I'm suggesting instead that the affinities and diversities of a group of artists in residence could – and perhaps should – be summoned also to produce collective intelligence towards societal change. Perhaps they could recognise the socio-political potential for a temporary community of residents to incubate strategies for sustainable living that might later be replicated outside the incubator.

Fundamentally, all such institutions share ideals of freedom for art and artists, along with their necessary, albeit temporary removal and protection from daily life. Therefore, as soon as the ghost of ideology – or better, socio-political responsibility – is invoked, many stakeholders may become wary of what I'm saying. At the same time, it is interesting to note that artist residencies often organise community-oriented, educational programmes that institute social engagement and shape local policies, while depending on somewhat politicised funding arrangements based on a far from neutral *quid pro quo*.

Another point against my argument upholds the clear distinction between the artwork and the artist. Those invested in the arts – myself included – may tend to see the creation of meaning, the making sense of the world, and the imagination of new worlds as foundational and intrinsic to the power of the artwork rather than the artist. In that case, why push for a bunch of artists to act as collective intelligence instead of simply facilitating the production of individual artistic intelligence? First, because a collective intelligence of artists is composed by individual artistic ways of knowing and would certainly not exclude the production of art. Second, because societal development is urgent, and because difficult and complex issues are better resolved through collaboration. We clearly need all the intelligence we can get if we are to imagine viable solutions to our shared problems.

This brings me to another dichotomy or paradox that would deserve an entire essay. It is impossible to talk about communal living or about artist residencies and their relationship to twentieth-century experiments in cohabitation without noting that most residencies are rooted in anti-neoliberal ideas that value radical hospitality, sharing and togethering. In short, they embody the fundamental ideas of commonism.[1]

In residencies space, facilities, food and other resources are usually shared, while social interaction tends towards collaboration. (In rural residencies this often includes the land or a garden as the smallest share

1 The word 'commonism' is used here in reference to the definition given by the artist Nico Dockx and the sociologist Pascal Gielen in *Commonism: A New Aesthetics of the Real* (Amsterdam: Valiz, 2018). They write: 'After half a century of neoliberalism, a new radical, practice-based ideology is making its way from the margins: commonism, with an o in the middle. It is based on the values of sharing, common (intellectual) ownership and new social co-operations. Commoners assert that social relationships can replace money (contract) relationships. They advocate solidarity and they trust in peer-to-peer relationships to develop new ways of production.'

of the ecological commons.) The very idea of spending time in a communal residency suggests some kind of alignment with the ideals of collectivity and community that in turn underpin commonism's ideals of collective ownership and communal accessibility of resources at large – beyond the traditional commons.

But it is one thing is to enact commonism in our daily interactions with other residents and staff, another to work towards the creation of a cultural common within and around that residency and another still to work towards artistic commoning in general. As we have seen, commonist aesthetics and behaviours are often a *conditio sine qua non* for anyone involved with artist residencies, but broader ideas of the cultural commons or artistic commoning clash with the hyper-capitalist market rules that still govern the arts sector on which artist residencies inevitably rely.

This is the possible paradox: artist residencies properly belong to a tradition of experimental cohabitation and working that is infused with explicitly political intentions, yet today, in prioritising art and artists' freedom, they tend to downplay any heavy-duty political project. When the valuable practice – I would even like to say rehearsal – of intersectional sustainable co-living and co-working does occur in artist residencies, it isn't necessarily the result of some overarching institutional vision, but rather a by-product of the residents' self-determination in their temporary commonality. Indeed I believe this political undercurrent could be more emphatically abetted by explicit social, spatial, ethical and moral – and therefore political – strategies put in place by the residencies themselves.

I have described the residency as a 'collective intelligence', but another possibility would be to consider it a specific type of 'assemblage'[2] or even 'assembly'. Such words are a way to focus our attention on the ever-changing ecosystem of human and non-human agents that make up the temporary community of artist residencies and to the ways in which they might productively operate. The diversity and breadth of skills and talents required to run any kind of commune amount to an assemblage – that is, an intentionally assembled group of agents that ensures both the smooth running of the place and the upholding of its vision. In an artist residency this assemblage might be 'curated' around a theme, a set of parameters or a centre of attention. Otherwise it is the complex result of the reciprocal, gravitational pull of shared cultures, politics, ethics and ideals happening between resident and residency. In my opinion, all assemblages can yield collective intelligence as soon as they assemble themselves around a specific question or issue.

However, the only event that formally looks like an assembly in a standard artist residency is the typical portfolio presentation or ideas-sharing meeting – maybe once a day or once a week, that depends. Apart from this particularly formalised moment, the collective intelligence of the residency assemblage

2 The concept of 'assemblage' that I refer to here was originated by the philosophers Gilles Deleuze and Félix Guattari in *A Thousand Plateaus* (1980), and somewhat defined by Deleuze in conversation with the journalist Claire Parnet in 1987: 'What is an assemblage? It is a multiplicity which is made up of many heterogeneous terms and which establishes liaisons, relations between them, across ages, sexes and reigns – different natures. Thus, the assemblage's only unity is that of a co-functioning: it is a symbiosis, a "sympathy". It is never filiations which are important, but alliances, alloys; these are not successions, lines of descent, but contagions, epidemics, the wind.' (Quoted in Manuel DeLanda, *Assemblage Theory* (Edinburgh University Press, 2016), p. 1.) That said, my understanding of the term 'assemblage' is also indebted to the Assemblage Theory outlined by Manuel DeLanda in *A New Philosophy of Society: Assemblage Theory and Social Complexity* (London: Continuum, 2006) and in *Assemblage Theory* (Edinburgh University Press, 2016). Furthermore, I have been fascinated by the archaeologist Yannis Hamilakis's notion of 'sensorial assemblages', whereby he suggests that 'sensoriality and affectivity, memory and multi-temporality are key features of assemblage thinking, and that assemblages also imply certain political effects'. Yannis Hamilakis, 'Sensorial Assemblages: Affect, Memory and Temporality in Assemblage Thinking', *Cambridge Archaeological Journal* 27:1 (2017), pp. 169–182.

is working away unnoticed, constantly reconfiguring the dynamics of the group and the place. The artist residency is a microcosm of society with benefits like no other cultural form of togethering. Its prevailing science is artistic intelligence, and its common denominator is the willingness to live and work in proximity to a number of relatable yet diverse agents for a defined period of time.

This rich net of new relations can make or break many residency experiences – more so than staff, landscape or facilities. What would happen if sustainable cohabitation were positioned at the forefront of institutional vision and strategy rather than happening in the background? Or if it were at least recognised in all its power and potential? What would we discover if we put artistic intelligence to use, towards more deliberate and iterative investigations into communal living and working? I'm not proposing to turn artist residencies into laboratories of social engineering and architecture, where the artists are instrumentalised for the sake of some higher project, or where their free individual work practice is compromised. Yet given that large parts of the cultural world are already preoccupied with imagining a more sustainable, just and equal future, and that the number of artist residencies is increasing to meet the demand for more protected and controllable socio-spatial arrangements, I think now is the time to accentuate with language, policies and resources what is already happening of its own accord.

I would like to end with another difficult question. What is the public value of artist residencies? Mainstream economic theory uses the 60-year-old definition of public goods as market failures that need to be corrected by the government. Art and culture may be convincingly, if simplistically, defined as both private and public goods. One only needs to look at national museums and art fairs, respectively. Generally speaking, artist residencies are financially supported by both the government and the market, and arguably produce both private and public value. That is, they facilitate the direct and indirect production of cultural products, while providing cultural services to a number of audiences and stakeholders, either inside or outside the arts arena. It is difficult to disentangle the question of public value from the service that artist residencies typically provide to the private sector. They facilitate the production of goods, often through the use of public money, that may end up circulating in the market: sculptures, books, scripts, compositions.

Nevertheless, some possible answers to my question might be: knowledge production and exchange; cultural diplomacy; psychological, social, professional and spiritual respite for artists, creative practitioners and researchers; national prestige; a contribution to local economies and community-building. Ironically, it is much easier to measure the economic value that artist residencies produce by influencing artists' careers and delivering impact on their local communities, than it is to prove their worth in terms of collective and common value. That would amount to defining and acknowledging all the significant positive externalities of art and culture.

In sum, artist residencies are fragile institutions, continuously compromising between independence, market forces, public agendas and local politics to justify their existence. My aim here is not to mount the case for a blanket recognition of art as a public need or for an instrumentalisation of artists' work, but simply to suggest that artist residencies may facilitate the production of public value by embracing their political potential as laboratories of intersectional sustainability in these unsustainable times.

What Next?

Miriam
La Rosa

Art Residences, Time Travelling and Ostension

Dr. Miriam La Rosa is a Sicilian-born curator, researcher and award-winning writer based in Naarm/Melbourne, Australia, with over 15 years of experience in the arts field. She holds a PhD from the University of Melbourne and has investigated notions of gift-exchange and host-guest relationships in cross-cultural residencies. Dr. La Rosa is currently Curator at the City of Greater Dandenong, overseeing the exhibition program at Walker Street Gallery and Arts Centre and the upcoming Dandenong New Art (DNA) Gallery. Previously she served as the Art Projects & Research Manager at Agency, supporting Indigenous-led initiatives in the arts, cultural and environmental sector. She has curated over 20 exhibitions, about 15 art residency initiatives and many public events, contributing to collaborative research projects in Italy, France, Spain, the Netherlands, the UK, Germany, Mexico and Australia. Dr. La Rosa is Treasurer of the International Association of Art Critics (AICA) Australia and a founding member of ARRC – Art Residency Research Collective. Her work has been published in various curatorial and academic journals, showcasing her commitment to the global discourse in contemporary art.

INTRODUCTION[1]

In this essay I explore the changing relationship between art residencies and ostension, the act of showing and displaying something. In my work on residencies, I argue that the relational and contextual value of residency programs is delimited by the difficulty and delicacy of negotiated interactions between resident artists and hosts – individuals as well as places.[2] A compelling characteristic of residencies is that their success depends on the potential of art to mediate the differences between host and guest. In this mediation, art can be transacted as a gift with professional as much as personal connotations.

Prior to the eruption of the Covid-19 pandemic, art residencies were widely associated with geographical movement and imbricated with the metaphor of the journey. Whether one decides to follow a conventional narrative, which places the origins of residencies in the seventeenth century and within the geopolitical borders of Europe, or seeks alternative routes to understand them, their history is intrinsically related to that of mobility.[3] Once the global perception of movement and place was challenged, and physical travel became less attainable, the very definition of an art residency required rethinking. What can be left of a residency when travelling is no longer an option?

The urgency of this question was addressed in Covid-era international forums by residency specialist organisations such as Res Artis, Transartists and Arquetopia Foundation.[4] Driving these discussions was mainly a desire to find solutions rather than examine the nature or ontology of residencies. The proposed answer was, predictably, the virtual residency. Communication technologies and, more recently, digital technologies proliferated well before the Coronavirus crisis took place. However, their possibility in residencies and the wider arts industry had remained relatively unexplored, largely confined to rethinking the archive and some experimental art practices. Then, during enforced isolation, all art and its fruition went online, uncovering for many new ways and forms of experience. In other words, whilst digital sharing and exchange had previously occurred in the residency field, in 2020 and 2021 the great majority of these interactions became exclusively so.[5] Showing, displaying and pinpointing – what I here call ostension – began to play a key

1 A version of this now revised article was previously published
in *OBOE Journal*. See Miriam La Rosa, 'New Start: The Marrgu
Residency Program and the Future of Showing', *OBOE Journal* 2,
no. 1 (2021), pp. 55–70.

2 See Miriam La Rosa, 'Guests, Hosts, Ghosts: Art Residencies
and Cross-Cultural Exchange' (The University of Melbourne,
2023).

3 A concise history of residencies has been circulated through
residencies web directories such as Res Artis and Transartists.
A 2019 anthology, edited by Taru Elfving, Pascal Gielen and
Irmeli Kokko, is the first attempt to expand upon this narrative
by giving a voice to different programmes, art practitioners
and academics from different regions. See Taru Elfving, Pascal
Gielen and Irmeli Kokko (eds), *Contemporary Artist Residencies:
Reclaiming Time and Space* (Amsterdam: Valiz, 2019). For a con-
cise account of the history of residencies, see also Miriam La
Rosa, 'Introduction', in *In Transition: The Artistic and Curatorial
Residency*, Margarida B. Amorim, Alejandro Ball, Miriam La Rosa
and Stefania Sorrentino (eds) (London: CtC Press Ltd, 2015). In
his doctoral research project at the Edinburgh College of Art,
Pau Catà has written what he termed an alternative proto-history of residencies with a focus on artists' mobility in the North
African region, which is an invaluable contribution to challenge
the normative and Western-centred history on residencies
circulated to date. See Pau Catà, 'Moving Knowledges: Towards
a Speculative Arab Art Residency Proto-History' (Edinburgh
College of Art, Scotland, 2021).

4 Between September and October 2020, Res Artis: Worldwide
Network of Arts Residencies and IASPIS, the Swedish Arts
Grants Committee's International Programme for Visual and
Applied Artists, with the support of Creative Victoria, presented
a free series of five webinars titled *Residencies in Challenging
Times*. Available at: https://resartis.org/2020/08/27/residen-
cies-in-challenging-times/ (accessed in February 2024). From
3 June to 27 July 2020, Arquetopia Foundation run *The End
of the Grand Tour? Virtual Symposium on Artist Residencies:
Future, Place and State*. Available at: https:// www.arquetopia.
org (accessed in February 2024). About one year after, Res Artis
held its annual conference entitled *Defining the New Decade* (8,
10–11 and 14, 16–17 September 2021) for the first time fully online, which had a strong focus on digital residencies and where I
was invited to present. Available at: https://resartis.org/res-ar-
tis-conferences/past-conferences/bangkok-2021/?swcfpc=1
(accessed in February 2024).

5 In stating this, it is important to mention that during lockdown,
some artworks remained blocked inside studios and galleries
with no audiences to visit them, not even online. The philosopher Jean-Paul Sartre would argue that this art is *not there*
with no one being able to experience it. He would also say that
through the act of seeing and experiencing art, visitors would
somewhat take it away, steal it, with their memory. See: Mark
Carroll, '"It Is": Reflections on the Role of Music in Sartre's *La
Nausée*', *Music & Letters* 87, no. 3 (2006), pp. 398–407. Is this
another form of travelling art?

role. One may object that the act of presenting is a common trait of any residency project. Here, I argue otherwise and suggest that the shift to online engagement leads to a more complex degree of ostension, which I analyse in depth. I further ask: what do these thoughts on ostension say about residencies after the pandemic?

This article considers the implications and potentials of travelling art, from the art historical phenomenon of Mail Art to the experimentations and the limitations triggered from 2020 onwards, which led to some transformations in the understanding of the art residency. I illustrate my view with a reference to the experience and work of the Art Residency Research Collective (ARRC), a team of researchers, artists, curators and writers that I'm part of, united in study around art residencies' shifting practices. Drawing from ARRC and a former exchange project, I introduce the hybrid residency, a combination of in-real-life and virtual engagement, which provides a case for assessing the current developments of residencies in the (post-)pandemic era.

TRAVELLING ART

6 For an account of this diversity, visit Res Artis (https://resartis.org) or TransArtists (https://www. transartists.org) (accessed in February 2024).

7 Vytautas Michelkevi-čius, *Mapping Artistic Research: Towards a Diagrammatic Knowing* (Vilnius Academy of Arts Press, 2018).

Today the field of residencies is extremely wide and diversified, with programs proliferating in the most disparate locations: from public and institutional venues to private and experimental settings.[6] Assumptions tending towards homogenisation are not possible, nor are they useful. Yet for many artists a 'residency' is a research or production phase within their practice, not necessarily geared towards the display of art. If the latter occurs, it does so as a consequence and result of the residency experience.[7] Online residencies can serve the same purpose, focusing on research rather than display. However, participants also find themselves engaged in a compulsory process of demonstration and exhibition that is both dictated and mediated by the nature of digital connection and the surface of the screen. Virtual infrastructures such as Zoom, Google or Instagram can serve as instruments for artists to realise their exchanges. These tools are inherently based on the ostensive condition of art: the (live) exhibition of concepts, images and in-progress works, unfolding alongside an equally curated presentation of identity and sense of place.

A question that emerges is the nature of the gift, in relation to the virtual. During the 2020–21 lockdowns that the pandemic activated in many parts of the world, Zoom proved to be a powerful medium for maintaining existing kin relations from a distance. Is this, however, also the case for expanding kin relations? And to what extent does the virtual increase and frustrate, rather than satisfy, the desire of knowing the other? We can argue that new relations can also be established virtually, but in a necessarily different, (and incorporeal) way.

In 2020, I became involved with ARRC. Our group was born out of curiosity as much as necessity. The former concerned the members' shared research interest in residencies, while the latter was dictated by our (dis)locations: Pau Catà in Barcelona, Morag Iles in Newcastle upon Tyne, Patricia Healy McMeans in Minneapolis, Angela Serino in Amsterdam and I in Naarm/Melbourne. Until today, connecting online is the only viable way for us to meet regularly, across different regions and time zones. What started as a singular meeting in anticipation of the 2020 Saari Summer Well in Finland progressively became a fortnightly appointment. Arguably, it became an ongoing residency in itself, a space for learning, study and debate as much as for friendship, co-creation and care.

Drawing from our individual research focuses, we developed a series of macro issues and sub-questions around residencies, which we later grouped under the headings of 'time, place, otherness, virtuality and ecology'. They read as follows:

Time: How can a residency take into account and respect the time of life, the time of the artist, of the artwork and of the institution? How can art residencies as spaces still exist within art residencies as time? Are other times, those lost in memory, still speaking to us?

Place: What kinds of experiences do artists need from a residency, and what is their affect? What does radical hospitality and slow immersion look like inside a lived residency, and how can we re-imagine the relevance of place and habitus in the new hybridised art residency model?

Otherness: How do we deconstruct the current thinking around residencies and develop a more inclusive understanding of the residency format? How do art residencies consider the specificities of remote and non-urban territories? How do they engage Indigenous knowledges and cultures?

Virtuality: If the journey as physical movement is replaced, how might that affect the essence of residency, as disruption of one's habitus? Can the monopoly of the presence, so often performed through the art residency, be challenged? Does the virtual–analogue binary still apply? Who holds the digital space and takes care of it? What is the significance of arrival and departure?

Ecology: What are the implications of late pandemic and climate crisis conditions on residencies, and how can we find a path forward that is equitable and ethical? How can we challenge rather than reproduce the existing extractive/fossil economy?[8]

8 See ARRC: https://arrcsite.org
(accessed in February 2024).

These questions led us to conceive two types of activities that we now employ to work together. 'External Movements' signify our interaction with the world outside of our core group, through, for instance, participation in workshops, public discussions and art projects. 'Internal Gestures' comprise practices and experiments we develop with one another, through both virtual connection (during our online meetings) and IRL engagement (exchange with an emphasis on our individual surroundings). The latter, in particular, has translated into the sending of instructions and documents (thoughts in a box) via the postal service, as each of us has crafted a secret action, a ritual, in response to one of the macro issues mentioned above.

Unlike the fast, digital connection of our Zoom meetings, our boxes travel slowly and get trapped. They stop at customs and get delayed because of the overtaking pace of our commitments and daily life. They are inefficient but also essential for enhancing and realising the meaning of our residency. They invite us to travel, with time.

A relevant predecessor to this practice, embodying the twofold purpose of communication through travel and connection through art, is Mail Art: the historical precursor of internet art or net.art. Art historians have outlined its chronology in distinct periods.[9] Deemed to have originated in works by Marcel Duchamp, Kurt Schwitters and the Italian Futurists, Mail Art gained momentum in the 1960s when artists like Ray Johnson and Edward M. Plunkett began to use the mail service as an official form of artistic correspondence. However, in a text published in *Art Journal* in 1977, Plunkett notes that the art of correspondence goes back to primordial times, crediting queen Cleopatra as the first one to inaugurate it – when she wrapped herself into a rug to be sent as a surprise to Julius Caesar.[10] Following his line of thought, further prehistoric instances of this will to travel, trade and exchange can be dated back to the Palaeolithic age, with the over 200 Venus figurines retrieved throughout Europe and Asia. The materials and visual characteristics of the little statues suggest that they might have been objects of trade or, at least, subject to travelling.[11]

In the Australian context, where I am based, there are accounts of pre-colonial Aboriginal ancestral objects (what we now call art) being taken on tours. The *Message Stick* story painted by Regina Pilawuk Wilson, a Ngan'gikurunggurr woman and senior artist from Peppimenarti (Northern Territory, Australia), is an example.[12] Wilson's work embodies a form of visual communication that her ancestors employed during their trade-related travelling. As Aboriginal artists responded to the colonial demand for their art, anthropologists and later tourists functioned as couriers to distant markets.[13]

9 Laura Dunkin-Hubby, 'A Brief History of Mail Art's Engagement with Craft (c. 1950–2014)', *Journal of Modern Craft* 9, no. 1 (2016), pp. 35–54.

10 https://artpool.hu/Ray/Publications/Plunkett.html (accessed in February 2024).

11 Olga Soffer, James M. Adovasio, and David C. Hyland, 'The "Venus" Figurines: Textiles, Basketry, Gender, and Status in the Upper Paleolithic', *Current Anthropology* 41, no. 4 (2000), pp. 511–37. See also John Noble Wilford, '"Venus" Figurines from Ice Age Rediscovered in an Antique Shop', in *The New York Times* 1 February 1994. Available at: https://www.nytimes.com/1994/02/01/science/venus-figurines- from-ice-age-rediscovered-in-an-antique-shop.html (accessed in February 2024). There have been several studies on the purpose and function of the Venus figurines. In 2020, a discovery concluded that they might have helped pre-historic Europeans to survive the Ice Age. Garry Shaw, 'Voluptuous Venus Figurines May Have Helped Prehistoric Europeans Survive the Ice Age', *The Art Newspaper* 3 December 2020. Available at: https://www.theartnewspaper.com/news/voluptuous-venus-figurines- may-have-helped-prehistoric-europeans-survive-the-ice-age (accessed in February 2024).

12 For an analysis of Regina Pilawuk Wilson's work, see Harriet Fesq, 'Wupun/Warrgadi: Ngan'gi Fibre and the Art of Peppimenarti' (University of Sydney, 2013).

13 Ian McLean, *Rattling Spears: A History of Indigenous Australian Art* (London: Reaktion Books, 2016).

Perhaps Plunkett's awareness of the deep-time genealogy of travelling art gave him the confidence to challenge normative, museum-specific contemporary art practices, as in 1962
he founded the New York Correspondence School (also referred
to as Correspondance), active until 1975.[14] In the 1960s George
Maciunas and the Fluxus artists also used the post to send ideas,
thoughts and artistic prompts to each other, creating an international network at a time when the internet was not an option. The
trend was then revisited in the 1990s. British curator Matthew
Higgs established Imprint, a project in which emerging artists
including Jeremy Deller, Martin Creed, Peter Doig, Chris Ofili and
Fiona Banner mailed provocative works to critics, curators and
other individuals associated with the art world.[15] The art historian and artist Laura Dunkin-Hubby has furthermore identified
what she names the latest 'era' (ca. 2000–14) in which Mail Art is
still operating, coexisting with the internet age.[16]

In the altered (art) world structure that the pandemic
created, some artists again chose the postal service as a means
for their work to move in a portable format.[17] However, the practice of art travelling instead of people, and through shipping, had
already been adopted before the pandemic by artists struggling
with the socio-political restrictions imposed by authoritarian
governments. A significant example is the work *Airmail Paintings*
by Chilean artist Eugenio Dittborn, developed in the 1970s during
the dictatorship in Chile as a series of paintings that could be
folded and sent abroad.[18] The scope of the project was to reach
out to the outside world, in the manner of a message in a bottle.
Similarly, a few decades later, the South Korean artist Kyungah
Ham began smuggling designs into North Korea, through helpers
based in Russia and China, to be translated into silk embroidery
made by a group of anonymous artisans. The finished works,
which were large scale representations of chandeliers, were
then trafficked back out of North Korea and displayed at galleries worldwide.[19]

These stories reinforce the point, core to this discussion,
that (travelling) art holds an incredible connective power among
individuals and cultures. Beyond the desire and need for communication, this connective power especially manifests itself
when people experience conditions of remoteness and isolation,
or when they live under enforced measures that restrict their

14 William S. Wilson, 'NY Correspondance School', *Art and Artists* I, no. 1 (1966). Available at: https:// www.warholstars.org/ray-johnson.html (accessed in February 2024).

15 In 2016 the Whitechapel Gallery, London, proposed an archival exhibition on the history of this endeavour, entitled *Imprint* 93 (19 March – 25 September 2016). Available at: https:// www. whitechapelgallery.org/exhibitions/ imprint-93/ (accessed in February 2024).

16 See Laura Dunkin-Hubby, 'A Brief History of Mail Art's Engagement with Craft (c. 1950– 2014)'.

17 Nanette Orly, 'How Artists Turned to the Postal Service', *Art Guide Australia* 2020. Available at: https://artguide.com.au/how-artists-turned-to-the-postal-service (accessed in February 2024).

18 The sociologist and critic Nelly Richard has written extensively in this regard. See Nelly Richard, *The Insubordination of Signs: Political Change, Cultural Transformation, and Poetics of the Crisis* (Durham, NC: Duke University Press, 2004).

19 David Segal, 'An Artist Unites North and South Korea, Stitch by Stitch', *The New York Times* 26 July 2018. Available at: https://www.nytimes. com/2018/07/26/arts/design/kyungah-ham-north-korea.html (accessed in February 2024).

freedom of movement and expression – or simply want to challenge normative, site-specific practices of established institutions and art centres.

Before ARRC, I experimented with this concept in a project developed for the Marrgu Residency Program, an Indigenous-led initiative of Durrmu Arts in Peppimenarti, which I have discussed elsewhere.[20] This program was launched in 2018 by Durrmu Arts' Cultural Director Regina Pilawuk Wilson to provide artists based in Peppimenarti with an opportunity to engage with fellow creative practitioners directly on Country. It aimed to encourage intercultural exchange, knowledge sharing and relationship building between remote and urban communities, local and international artists, and Indigenous and non-Indigenous cultural practices. In the Ngan'gi language the word *marrgu* means 'knowledge sharing' as well as 'new start'. Two years after its inception, and with the onset of the Covid-19 pandemic, Marrgu adapted to a virtual format, using technology to connect participants.

The residency I was invited to facilitate involved three artists: Regina Pilawuk Wilson, the Yindjibarndi artist Katie West and the Malaysian-born, Aotearoa-raised and Australia-based artist Fayen d'Evie. Each descending from different cultures and residing in different places. Each based in a different Indigenous Country and State of Australia: Ngan'gikurunggurr Country, Northern Territory (Regina); Noongar Ballardong Boodja, Western Australia (Katie); and Dja Dja Wurrung Country, Victoria (Fayen). The associations between their practices are not obvious, although Katie and Fayen have an ongoing artistic collaboration.[21] They experiment with different mediums to realise large-scale textile installations (Katie) and works that investigate touch, movement, language and sound (Fayen). Regina is then a master weaver and painter. What linked them in the context of this residency was an interest in tactility and history and the use of materials that derive from their surroundings, be they stories, objects or, for Regina and Katie in particular, natural fibres and colours. Their work shares a dedicated engagement with the places that host them.

The plan was for them to connect on virtual platforms, posting images of their daily art practice, videos and field/voice recordings of their walks in a virtual diary. Showing, displaying and pinpointing – an ostension – were core features of the project. Yet, the initial proposal alone, a digital residency, was not sufficient to generate a meaningful experience. A difference in time zone and in each artist's relationship with technology as well as the diversity of their commitments, which had grown in lockdown, slowed the pace of the encounter. This was a valuable and realistic outcome that mirrored the spirit of the time, while also (and alas) obstructing a timely realisation of the exchange. Meetings would be cancelled, postponed, the flow interrupted. Therefore the artists were later encouraged to re-think, together, the format of their residency. To counteract a lack of physical movement, they decided to send extracts from their 'bush studios', postcards and small gifts to one another through the postal service. Regina sent her local *merrepen* (sand palm fibres) to Fayen and Katie, for them to practice weaving during their online meetings. Fayen sent a series of paper cuts from one of her works to Regina. She painted over these pages and mailed them back to both Fayen and Katie. An exchange of material and immaterial gifts was now at stake in the project, which had progressively become a hybrid residency to serve the intentions and desires of the participants better. Albeit originating online, this three-way residency found in the exchange of art (remnants, intimate stories and prompts) a successful and indispensable feature for its manifestation. A collective work, a sound piece, was developed at the conclusion of the activities.

In both cases, those of Marrgu and ARRC, time-travelling art across the points on the map inhabited by the participants, proved helpful for superseding the absence of physical proximity. The projects gifted something that comes directly from the hands, and the worlds, of the others involved. Both dimensions, the virtual and physical – the mediated presentation through a screen and the full experience in real time and space – are as important in hybrid residencies as they are in relation to one another. With these thoughts in mind, let us delve deeper into the metalevel of exchange.

20 See Miriam La Rosa, 'New Start: The Marrgu Residency Program and the Future of Showing'.

21 See *Museum Incognita*, available at: https://www.museumincognita.space (accessed in February 2024).

OSTENSION

The notion of ostension is employed in communication theory to address the intention to transmit something. It has been widely discussed in the fields of philosophy and linguistics by, among others, Ludwig Wittgenstein and Umberto Eco. It has also been applied to folklore studies by, for instance, John H. McDowell.[22] The latter frames ostension as a counterpart to iconicity (representation) and a vehicle to generate what he names 'a narrative epiphany', which provides 'a virtual encounter with experience'.[23] Whereas an icon represents – symbolises and stands for – something else, a narrative epiphany *presents*. It offers a virtual encounter with the experience in the sense that it evokes and creates the illusion of ostension, of the experience itself, including audiences as participants in the event rather than spectators of it.

From a semiotic perspective, however, one can argue that everything is perceived as a sign. As the philosopher Jacques Derrida would put it, we are always imagining that moment when a foot leaves its print on the sand but all we are left to look at is the print, the trace, on the sand.[24]

Speaking of ostensive definitions, Wittgenstein denied that the meaning of a word can be conveyed by the action of pointing at, displaying, or showing the thing a word refers to. For the philosopher, a pre-existing knowledge of the meaning of the thing itself is mandatory for understanding any example that is being provided. It follows that meaning is given by the *experience* of something. The understanding of a word's meaning follows the experience of the thing the word stands for. To say it otherwise, showing cannot connect to meaning but it is, at most, an association between written and spoken word.[25] The use we make of language, then, can affect the perception we have of reality.

The driving message of John Berger's *Ways of Seeing* is that the act of seeing precedes words while showing the opposite, that we see with signs. As the art critic highlights, language and narrative have the power to frame reality in exclusive and exclusionary ways. In support of his claims Berger brings forward different case studies: the history and meaning of the nude as the representation and presentation of women in art, which subtends a male-centric view of the world, the tradition of oil painting as the medium to embody and signify possession; and the role of advertising in depicting the ultimate consumerist desire.[26]

In art terms, these concerns suggest a double implication. On the one hand, exhibitions are agents that either reinforce or challenge a world one is already familiar with. They are like a work of fiction in that they create counter-worlds, which can only be understood from within our own experiences. On the other hand, they can also be used in demagogic as well as subversive ways. Think of the impact of mega-exhibitions such as biennials, triennials and Documenta on the definition of contemporary art, and on shaping the collective view of history and power, or think of collection displays – almost all museum displays in twentieth-century Europe and the United States – that have privileged a Western worldview. Think then, as a counterpart, of exhibitions that have attempted to rewrite history by proposing previously overlooked and suppressed narratives. An example is the 22nd Biennale of Sydney | *NIRIN* (2020). With its unprecedented representation of Indigenous practitioners from across the globe, it exemplifies the ostensive recognition of otherwise marginalised voices.[27]

22 The earliest use of the phrase 'ostensive definition' can be found in the 1920s, in the work of the logician William Ernest Johnson. See Ludwig Wittgenstein, *Tractatus Logico-Philosophicus* (London: Keagan Paul, 2014 [1922]).; Umberto Eco, *A Theory of Semiotics* (Bloomington: Indiana University Press, 1976).

23 John H. McDowell, 'Beyond Iconicity: Ostension in Kamsá Mythic Narrative', *Journal of the Folklore Institute* 19, no. 2/3 (1982), p. 127.

24 Jacques Derrida, *Archive Fever: A Freudian Impression* (University of Chicago Press, 1996).

25 Ludwig Wittgenstein and G. E. M. Anscombe, *Philosophical Investigations* (Hoboken, NJ: Blackwell, 1963).

26 John Berger, *Ways of Seeing* (London and New York: British Broadcasting Corporation and Penguin Books, 2000).

27 The 22nd Biennale of Sydney | *NIRIN* (14 March – 6 September 2020), https://www.biennaleofsydney. art/archive/22nd-biennale-sydney-nirin/ (accessed in February 2024).

How do such considerations inform the theme of residencies? In being based on, and defined by, the experience of sharing while being in a place, residencies are platforms that establish meaning and do not function in an ostensive way. They do not *present* an experience of art (an ostension) but rather *are* experiences of art in a set space and in real time. To be a resident means to reside, live in and actively engage with a place. Digital residencies, however, initiate a necessary relationship with the ostensive for the politics of displaying and are deeply entrenched within the structure of virtual connectivity. An online encounter with art demands a different level of action than a physical one, whereby, complying with the digital language, artists present their work in combination with their inclinations, inspirations, political views and personal beliefs. Yet, they are still bound by the ostensible, or apparent, authority and limits of the platform.[28]

As the media scholar Marshall McLuhan memorably argued, the medium delimits the message.[29] Digital connectivity demystifies and re-mystifies the existing art it reproduces, taking it down from its former pedestal. It de-sacralises the meaning of art with the same power, for example, as when the art museum removed sacred art from churches and re-presented it in an aestheticised space, or as when the book fixed performed oral stories in the form of text. The digital medium sets new limits on the meaning and gift exchange of the art. What do platforms such as Zoom and Google Meet contribute to the host–guest relationship and to hospitality?

Digital residencies and tools problematise McDowell's notion of virtual ostension. They re-present embodied experience as a screen-mediated interaction, defined by the semiotics of the screen and the software. For the literary critic Roland Barthes this is the structure of myth.[30] Real-time events occur in parallel universes between which delimited digital re-presentation is exchanged, as if through a wormhole. The digital gives the ostensive the possibility to occur in multiple registers at the same time, that is, with different screens and audio/video channels, which complicate the meaning of the work (of art) involved in the act of showing. Since digital residents are not physically present in the same place and at the same time, they provide extracts, examples of their experience, in order to allow their fellow participants to sample aspects of them.

Art, like language, has always travelled through its reproduction, but as Walter Benjamin argued, in his seminal text *The Work of Art in the Age of Mechanical Reproduction*, its acceleration by mechanical reproduction (photographic and print technology) has fundamentally altered how art is experienced.[31] This idea is at the heart of Berger's thought. The restrictions of the pandemic were the perfect environment for exponentially enhancing the power of digital imagery, but to what effect on the experience of art and residencies themselves? How is this process reforming the possibilities of both residencies and art?

The etymology of ostension (from the Latin verb *ostendo, ostendere, ostendi, ostensus*) refers to pointing out, making clear, displaying, exhibiting, revealing or showing. The meaning of the term can be further understood by looking at the connotation of its relatives, the adjectives 'ostensive' (which stands

28　A 2021 article in *The Art Newspaper* reported the story of Don't Delete Art, a New York-based advocacy group that has shared a guide for artists to circumvent censorship of their works on social media platform such as Facebook and Instagram. These instructions on how to self-censor and pixelate images or employ hashtags wisely came after hundreds of artists protested that their works were being frequently removed from these platforms, and their complaints ignored. The story also speaks to the inherent capacity of artists to bypass limits in a creative way, be this in the IRL or digital world. Gareth Harris, 'Censored? Shadowbanned? Deleted? Here Is a Guide for Artists on Social Media', *The Art Newspaper*. (16 March 2021). Available at: https://www.theartnewspaper.com/2021/03/16/censored-shadowbanned-deleted-here-is-a-guide-for-artists-on-social-media (accessed in February 2024).

29　Marshall McLuhan, *Understanding Media: The Extensions of Man* (New York: McGraw Hill, 1964).

30　The myth, for Barthes, is a mode of signification, a language that takes over reality. See Roland Barthes, *Mythologies* (Paris: Editions du Seuil, 1957).

31　See Walter Benjamin, *The Work of Art in the Age of Mechanical Reproduction* (transl. Harry Zohn) (London: Penguin, 2008 [1935]).

for: 'of, relating to' or 'constituting definition by exemplifying the thing or quality being defined') and ostensible (i.e. 'intended for display, open to view' but also 'being such in appearance, plausible rather than demonstrably true or real').[32]

These definitions lead to distinct, albeit interrelated, aspects and uses of ostension. While the first exemplifies the notion explored by McDowell, a counterpart to iconicity, the second also highlights a faculty of ostension (the ostensible) to function as an apparent vehicle for conveying, displaying a message (in the noun ostentation such appearance becomes a sign for the unnecessary or superficial, e.g., an excessive show of vanity or wealth). Think of the role of a lecturer: their authority (to teach) is ostensible in that it is conferred by an institution, which the student (the guest) accepts. A similar principle applies to the museum, whose authoritative role is given by the discourse of art as much as taken away by it. (Think of Institutional Critique.) To unpack this even further, we can refer to the legal use of ostension, where an 'ostensible authority' is a type of legal relationship between what are known as 'a principal' and 'an agent', and where the latter is conferred an ostensible (apparent yet effective) power, in the sense that their authority is based on perception and determined by the situation, an action, rather than a qualification (the agent *acts* in place of the principal).[33]

However, ostension also signifies concepts such as 'river mouth', 'doorway', 'entrance to the underworld', 'front door', and 'starting gate', derived from the same root of the verb, as the Latin noun *ostium, osti(i)*.[34] We can observe an etymological proximity between ostension and hosting, with the host being a door opener to the guest in their own home.

With the pandemic having created a crisis of ostension, but also an opportunity through the enhanced use of digital platforms, should the institutions formally dedicated to the presentation of art revaluate their mission and scope? Specifically for our field, what comes next for being in residence? The ongoing experience of ARRC suggests that the future of ostension for art practices in a globalised digital world can benefit from the new understanding we have gained of online connectivity. Whilst the value of physical travel and in-person exchange has its own dynamic than can (if only partially) be replicated by the semiotics of digital or other media forms, the geographical challenge proposed by the pandemic has forced us to explore the capacity of virtual interaction at a more intense level – and in a blend of analogue and digital modes.

CONCLUSION

In this article, I have attempted to provide an overview of the changing relationship between art residencies and ostension. I have addressed some of the issues that the post-2020 residency field is presented with. Among these issues, there is a crisis of showing, which goes hand in hand with a crisis of time and place. If an effective conclusion arrives at new questions for the future, I would ask: Has the pandemic challenged the ontology of residencies in ways that remind us of the purpose of art, that is, to signify? How can the enforced digitisation in the increased ostensive condition of the platforms for art (including in art residencies) remain beneficial? Can we begin to understand ostension as the act of hosting alongside showing? Mediation is, after all, a condition for hospitality (a residency) to occur. The same applies to the late pandemic age, which shows us that (art) travelling, with *both* showing and hosting, still happens; it just does so in a more intricate and complex ways.

32 *Merriam-Webster Online Dictionary*, https://
www.merriam-webster.com/dictionary/osten-
sive (accessed in February 2024).

33 Thomson Reuters, *Practical Law Glossary*,
https://uk.practicallaw.thomsonreuters.
com/w-014-6055?transitionType=
Default&contextData=(sc.Default)&first-
Page=true (accessed in February 2024).
See also Enid Campbell, 'Ostensible Authority
in Public Law', *Federal Law Review 27*,
no. 1 (1999).

34 *Online Etymology Dictionary*, https://www.
etymonline.com/word/ostensive (accessed in
February 2024).

The Field of

Irmeli Kokko Interviews

Constant Changes

Anna Kirveennummi, Futurist,

and Leena Kela, Artist and Director of the Saari Residence

Irmeli Kokko is an educator, writer and curator based in Helsinki. For the last 25 years, she has been active in the field of artist residencies as an organiser and expert. She holds an MA in cultural politics and art education from the University of Jyväskylä and has launched residency programmes such as HIAP, the Helsinki International Artist Programme (1999) and international residency progammes for artists from Finland (2003–07, with Frame, the Finnish Fund for Art Exchange, and 2005–08, with the Academy of Fine Arts, Uniarts, Helsinki and the Saastamoinen Foundation). Kokko has organised international symposia such as *My Journey: Research and Exchange* (Saari Residence, 2021) and *Residencies Reflected* (HIAP, with Taru Elfving and Juha Huuskonen, 2016), which resulted in the book *Contemporary Artist Residencies: Reclaiming Time and Space* (Amsterdam: Valiz, 2019) that she co-edited with Taru Elfving and Pascal Gielen.

Leena Kela is a performance artist, curator, residency director and researcher based in Mynämäki, Finland. She is Director of the Saari Residence in Mynämäki, Artistic Director of the New Performance Turku Biennale and a doctoral candidate at the Academy of Fine Arts, Uniarts, Helsinki. In her artistic work and research, Kela explores dialogues between corporeality and materiality in performance art. She has presented her performances internationally in festivals, events and exhibitions. Recent projects include the performance *Ghosts Among Us* at the *Performancear o Morir* festival in Mexico in 2024, the video *Islet Borewell* (in collaboration with artists Heini Aho and Eero Yli-Vakkuri) at the Helsinki Biennial in Helsinki in 2023 and the video exhibition *Rest of Us* at the Poikilo Art Museum in Kouvola in 2024, Nykyaika gallery in Tampere in 2023 and Kunsthalle Turku in 2022.

Dr. Anna Kirveennummi is a futurist based in Turku, Finland. She is Project Researcher at Finland Futures Research Centre at the University of Turku and has been involved in planning and developing the operations of the Saari Residence as a member of the advisory board from 2007. She holds a PhD from the School of History, Culture and Arts Studies of the University of Turku. In her doctoral thesis *An Invitation to Participate in Scientific Activity: Ethnographic Perspectives on Collaboration Practices in Multidisciplinary Questionnaire Activity* (in Finnish, 2023) she explored multi-actor collaboration practices and dialogues in scientific practices from an ethnographic perspective. Dr. Kirveennummi's interests include the futures of materiality, resources, practices and cultural interaction. Her most recent projects address the futures of the circular economy, food and universities.

IK

The Saari Residence embraces sustainability as one of its guiding operating principles. What exactly does the concept of sustainable development entail?

LK Sustainability and responsibility stand at the forefront of the values and practices that guide everything we do at the Saari Residence. As the Intergovernmental Panel on Climate Change stated in its sixth Assessment Report published in 2023, climate change poses an immediate threat to human well-being and planetary health. We have precious little time to take corrective action. We live and work in the midst of an environmental crisis. We cannot simply turn our backs and carry on with business as usual. We must actively seek solutions and embrace readiness to change.

An artist residency is a place where creative work and everyday life are intertwined. It offers artists a break from their daily routine and obligations, enabling them to delve deeper into making art. Residencies differ from all other art organisations in the unique respect that the participants not only work but also reside onsite, which offers a rare opportunity to propose and test out alternative ways of living. I recognise vast potential here. By inviting artists to slow down and reflect, a residency can lead to the discovery of entirely new approaches to living and working.

AK Sustainable development is a process steered by many actors and stakeholders. It is a balancing effort to intervene in the midst of constant change. Science and art can offer valuable perspectives to broaden our understanding of what sustainability means or could mean in relation to the environmental crisis. Finding a balance entails that we actively strive to build a more sustainable future by harnessing all available means to mitigate or prevent adverse impacts that our actions exert on the environment.

In the context of the Saari Residence, the concept of sustainability underlines the fact that Saari, which literally means 'island', cannot be an island separate from the rest of the world. The residency's events, participants and processes are all inextricably linked to topical issues, current needs, and ideas about the urgency of change.

IK On a general level, what kind of new practices could a sustainability mindset generate?

AK Through art and science we can push boundaries and employ a holistic, experimental approach that integrates multiple perspectives. Sustainability projects often tend to focus on one small area at a time, but there are also wider systemic entanglements to be addressed. We need to consider interactions between multiple factors. When changes and measures are introduced, it is important to evaluate their outcome, also in terms of exposure to further change. We must also take into account that there are things emerging, for which we may not have a name. We may not be able to see what they do. Experimentation can yield knowledge about mutual interactions and the fundamental workings of wider systems.

LK If the residency is built on sustainable pillars in its energy solutions, transport, food, recycling and use of materials – and if these practices are communicated clearly as part of the daily routine – this offers a solid foundation for gaining deeper insights. A residency can encourage artists to slow down, live sustainably and observe how the slowed-down pace affects the way they act and think. Fresh insights can arise through new knowledge, especially in combined effect with shared experiences and emotional engagement.

Sustainable development embraces not only ecological sustainability but also social, economic and psychological sustainability. Climate change exacerbates social inequality because its life-threatening impacts are distributed unevenly across the globe. While the West is primarily accountable for the world's climate-polluting emissions, its negative effects are felt most keenly in the Global South.

For decades, artist residencies have upheld the entitled status of Western artists who enjoy the financial privilege of being able to travel to different parts of the world. Artist residencies can advance social justice through positive discrimination, first by favouring artists from the Global South and second by paying a working grant for the duration of the residency as well as covering travel and visa expenses.

IK

Art and culture change with the times. Is sustainable
development such a sweeping force of change that it
is altering the very conditions of art production?

AK   The cultural forces of change are complex, but sustainability has
become a highly visible part of the process of change. Sustainability is nevertheless a tool in a process of development which
itself must be examined openly, reflexively and critically. What
are the best solutions in given situations, and when is it wisest
to refrain from intervention and simply let things unfold natu-
rally towards the desired outcome? It would be good if the circumstances of living and making art could be developed, so that
making the right choices would not be left solely to the artists as
individuals.

LK   As a performance artist, I have been thinking for some time about
adaptation and reduction as strategies for a more sustainable
practice. Could I reduce my productivity and work at a slower
pace, which would permit me to delve deeper? Is art primarily
about notching up accomplishments, or something else entirely?
My education coincided with a period of accelerating globalisation and digitalisation when cheap flights opened up the world.
We artists were immediately part of the international art scene
from the moment we graduated. We were expected to keep up a
prolific pace and perform around the world.

Today everyone can see how utterly unsustainable this
approach is, but unlearning takes time. Inactivity – resting – is
an emerging form of resistance among artists and cultural practitioners whose precarious status leaves them exhausted yet
incapable of resting. The constant struggle to make ends meet
depletes their energy and resources, leaving no time for recovery. Psychological sustainability should be recognised as a pillar of sustainability. For artists, this pillar could be strengthened
by providing sufficient financial resources and enough time to
recover and reflect.

IK

What kind of scenarios do you foresee
for the future practice of art?

AK For a researcher this is a big question, because there is nothing sure to be said about the future. The future is constantly being reshaped through our actions and interwoven changes, continuities, discontinuities and disruptions. To consciously build a better future, we must first identify and strengthen the networks that foster sustainability through joint action.

Futurists often speak of the future in terms of 'both and' rather than 'either or'. Indeed tomorrow increasingly presents itself as an open field of difficult choices. Many choices entail uncertainties and giving up habitual things, which might, perhaps emphasise the role of intuition in the future.

LK In the years to come, artists will be forced to work within evermore fragile structures. Even now, many artists are struggling to uphold existing standards of sustainability, as the support structures available to artists are either non-existent or rapidly crumbling, or too inflexible and inaccessible.

A strong spirit of solidarity is needed within the community to prevent rivalry amid intensifying competition for dwindling resources. In the future, who will be the lucky few entitled to fly to residencies on the other side of the world? Or will residencies become local rather than global? If so, how can we ensure the continued exchange of ideas and cross-cultural encounters?

Today we are already seeing rapid convergence of art and digitalisation. Media art used to be its own genre, but nowadays almost all art is somehow connected to digital media. Like climate change, digitalisation is a reality that is reshaping our existence and ways of making art. These things are indissolubly intertwined. It will be interesting to see what kind of new approaches and forms of art-making emerge from digitalisation and the sustainability revolution.

AK   What options will be open to those who wish to maintain dis-
       tance from the digital domain? As art converges increasingly
       with digital culture, we are likely to see future generations adopt-
       ing a diversifying array of strategies to disengage from the digital
       sphere of influence.

IK

At different times in history, artists have gravitated
by turns to urban or remote rural locations for various
reasons. Take for instance the rise of artist colonies
in nineteenth- and twentieth-century Europe, which
was largely a response to the negative impacts of
industrialisation and the longing to return to 'pure'
unpolluted nature. Another example is the wave of
exile artists and the resultant avant-garde hubs that
emerged during the first and second world wars.
        Cities again became hubs of creativity and
innovation during the globalisation trend in the 1980s
and 90s. Artists have sought creative inspiration in
varied locations – sometimes cities, sometimes the
wilderness – and preferences have changed in step
with wider social upheavals. What are the respective
roles of urban and rural residencies with respect to
sustainability?

AK   Urban and rural regions coexist as complex, ever-changing
       entities that cannot be fully separated from each other or
       summed up under a blanket definition. Rural areas have typically
       been agricultural production sites where cyclicity and seasonal-
       ity have played a visible role in the cultural landscape.
               The Saari Residence is located in a rural municipality that
       has some of the characteristics of a small town. The residence
       is surrounded by modernised food production and local gover-
       nance. There is still much about the rural landscape that appears
       to be unchanging. Fields and forests foster the idea of continuity.

But this continuity is only skin-deep, for rural regions, too, are adapting to sustainability-driven systemic change, which must be balanced against the struggle to earn a livelihood in a changing climate. Rural regions contend with complex environmental and production-related vulnerabilities, and a sweeping transformation process lies ahead inexorably.

LK   A rural residency offers artists the opportunity to slow down, observe nature and partake in coexistence with other-than-human species. Compared with urban settings, a rural residency is not the ideal place for expanding professional networks or keeping up with new trends. The main takeaway is instead the experience of the place itself and the peace it offers for concentrated work. The unique character of the changing seasons is one of the special highlights of the Saari Residence. We usually have snow early in the year, and during cold winters, the Baltic Sea freezes over so that you can cross the ice by foot to nearby islands. We are located next to one of Finland's major bird wetland areas, which attracts vast flocks of migratory birds and accompanying droves of birdwatchers to our village every spring and autumn.

Seasonality is also emphasised in our programme of ecological activities, which includes guided mushrooming, foraging and birdwatching, and the literature we recommend in our learning circle is designed to promote ecological awareness. The absence of light pollution can itself be a valuable experience; many artists have praised the darkness and silence as a significant highlight of their residency experience. Living in the countryside is not simply an existence of silent communion with nature, however. Agriculture and the use of natural resources is an integral part of rural life, and we examine these complex issues as part of our residency activities.

AK   Since the early days of the Saari Residence, residents have harnessed the site's natural surroundings and organic processes as part of their artistic work. It is difficult to anticipate how this might change in the future. What new kind of relationship with nature might artists express in years to come? What issues will they address? What uncertainties will they encounter concerning their own knowledge and skills? I'm reluctant to predict the future of art because the strength of art lies in its very unpredictability.

LK Ecological practices are revolutionising the ways in which art is made and presented. Many artists are re-evaluating their choice of materials and strategies for presenting their work. Ecology has also emerged as a prominent theme in the content of art, and temporality has become a central concept in the wake of the sustainability movement. Making art takes time: an artist needs time to observe, experiment, notice and discover.

   The sustainability transformation requires a holistic change in our habitual practices, and the production of art is no exception. A residency can offer the necessary time and space to engage in practices or work stages that might seem 'unproductive' to the casual observer. Adopting new ways of living and thinking is likewise a process that requires time and space. Doing nothing whatsoever can sometimes create space for new ideas, which is one of the essential conditions for creating art.

IK

The future is our collective concern. What contribution can residencies make to benefit the creators of art, art overall and thereby all of society?

AK An artist residency is a structured, human-made institution that offers a certain amount of permanence, space and resources for encounters and creative projects. As we discussed earlier, for the chosen or invited artists a residency signifies not only a place to work but also a space for simply existing, pausing to reflect and temporarily belonging to a community.

   In the future we should also consider the 'ripples' that the Saari Residence sends outwards, in the form of alternative practices and new ways of thinking, being, sensing and experiencing. These can spread not only into the immediate environment but wider within the art communities and networks. How could these alternative practices spread the idea of hope-building and the importance of speculative dreaming?

LK A residency can be a good place to conduct basic research into the fundaments of artmaking and artistic thinking. Project-oriented residencies are useful for this purpose, but retreat-type residencies that simply encourage free thought and experimentation enable a deeper 'back to basics' approach. As with all basic research, such delving may not necessarily yield revolutionary applications immediately, but it can build the foundations for later breakthroughs and insights.

We might even think of a residency as a kind of knowledge-gathering sensor. I have often wondered about the kind of knowledge that is generated in residencies. What exactly does this knowledge consist of? A residency experience revolves around interaction. This might mean interaction between the residents during the process of creating and discussing art and spending time together.

In a smaller residency, this might primarily mean interaction with the immediate environment and its local characteristics. When artists come together during a residency, diverse cultures, artistic practices and modes of knowing converge momentarily, after which they continue their existence elsewhere, but they leave their mark on the place itself as traces that become layered over the passing years.

The knowledge generated in residencies is disseminated through ripple effects and mycelial networks, eventually reverberating across the entire art field and, ideally, throughout society.

In addition to their art-enabling role, I believe residencies carry wider responsibility as actors within the local community. Even if a residency operates internationally, it is also a local operator. The Saari Residence has its own permanent staff member – a community artist – who is tasked with bridge-building between the residence and the local community. At some residences, community relations are upheld through open studios, discussion panels or even parties. In this way, the residence 'breathes' out and influences the local community through varied forms of artistic thinking.

AK   Indeed, many existing artistic and scientific practices will survive in the future, even if their thematic content changes radically. Art enables us to experience things anew over and over again, often from unconventional perspectives. Going forward, I hope that art will continue to attract a diverse spectrum of audiences, offering eye-opening insights and shake-ups that awaken new thoughts and feelings. Meanwhile, new technologies are altering many established practices and reshaping our environment and the nature of the encounters that take place within it.

     Hopefully artist residencies will remain a nexus of emancipating processes and meaningful encounters, offering artists a place for recovery, renewal and respite from the pressures of daily life. It would of course be ideal if even more people had the opportunity to create subsidised art. Various issues related to social justice and equality must therefore be addressed in rethinking how residencies can serve various future needs.

LK   Above all, I hope that artist residencies can carry on their work with assurance of continuity amid the ever-accelerating pace of change. Then again, the only thing that never changes is change itself, which is also true of art and residencies as art enablers. Even if artistic methods change as a result of the environmental crisis and digitalisation, I believe that one key thing will never change: artists will always need time, space and peace to work, along with platforms for interaction.

In the future, I hope to see artist residencies grow into something bigger than 'just' a place that offers time, space and practical support for the production of art. As hubs of artistic thought, residencies can serve as incubators for the broader evolution of the entire art field. The future mission of artist residencies and their growing responsibility in the socially equitable transition to sustainability is aptly expressed in the following aphorism penned by poet and Saari alumnus Jonimatti Joutsijärvi: 'No hatching, no hatchling.'

Inertia, Duration and the Significance of Oblivion:

Maria Hirvi-Ijäs

Artist Residencies as Agents of Cultural Sustainability

Dr. Maria Hirvi-Ijäs is an art historian, critic and researcher based in Helsinki. She holds a PhD from the University of Helsinki and is Associate Professor at the Institute of Art History at Åbo Akademi University in Turku, Finland. Dr. Hirvi is also Senior Researcher at the Center for Cultural Policy Research Cupore in Helsinki, focusing on cultural policy in the Nordic countries. Recent publications include *Visuaaliset taiteet Suomessa* (*Visual Arts in Finland*, in Finnish) with Sari Karttunen, Emmi Lahtinen, Vappu Renko and Sakarias Sokka (Helsinki: Cupore, 2023), *Kultursektorns återhämtning och förändring efter covid-19-pandemin* (*The Recovery and Change of the Cultural Sector after the Covid-19 Pandemic*, in Swedish) with Olli Jakonen (Copenhagen: Nordic Council of Ministers, 2023) and a monograph on the Finnish artist group Salong 3+ (Helsinki: Parvs Publishing, 2023).

1   This estimate is based on figures reported on the websites of Res Artis and Transartist.

2   See Riikka Suomi-Chande, *Perusteita ja lukuja residenssitoiminnasta. Vinkkejä ja tukea toiminnan aloittamiseen ja ylläpitoon* (Helsinki: Studio Foundation of the Artists' Association of Finland, 2021) and Riitta Heinämaa, *Suomalainen residenssitoiminta tänään – nykytilanne ja kehittämistarpeet* (Helsinki: Föreningen Konstsamfundet, 2020).

3   This term was used by Irmeli Kokko in the author invitation for this book, in an e-mail dated 6 June 2022.

4   See Gilles Deleuze and Félix Guattari, *A Thousand Plateaus: Capitalism & Schizophrenia* (transl. Brian Massumi) (Minneapolis: University of Minnesota Press, 1987).

In 2022 there were nearly 2,000 organisations listed in the global network of artist residencies, covering a wide spectrum in terms of their history, goals, profile and structure.[1] In Finland alone, over 100 residencies are estimated to operate, but their precise total number is unconfirmed, as is the exact definition of what officially constitutes an artist residency.[2] Historically, most residencies have been intended for professionals working in the field of the visual arts – this also being the most active user group – but multidisciplinary residences bridging various fields of art and science are also emerging as a popular alternative.

'Mycelial' is an illustrative description of the varied, diversified yet relatively invisible practices of artist residencies.[3] Mycelium is a concept used in botany to describe the growth of fungal threads. These tiny threads are slowly woven together in an invisible yet expansive underground network, sometimes popping up above ground in surprising new places. Cultural analysis has borrowed the term 'mycelial' from post-structuralist philosophy, which coined the concept of the 'rhizome' as a metaphor describing how seemingly distant or even unrelated entities are interwoven in complex networks of multiplicities, yielding significant fruits at unpredictable exit points.[4]

Artist residencies straddle a borderland between the public and non-public domains. They operate invisibly in the sense that they are self-contained units accessible only to those in artistic professions, and yet at the same time they form networks of collaboration born to serve specific professional needs.

The work that goes on within residencies is often invisible or inaccessible to outsiders until the 'fruit' emerges, sooner or later, whether as an artistic action, a cultural service or an art market commodity. Until the fruit is ripe, residencies are essentially like workshops, back-office functions or incubators – and sometimes it takes a long time before tangible results become visible.

Working inconspicuously without anyone noticing the immediate relevance of one's work can be challenging, especially in the face of contemporary expectations and the pressure to be constantly 'on show', delivering proof of the value and efficacy of one's work. In Finland, this has often resulted in artist residencies being forgotten and overlooked. Their important role is easily disregarded also in public debate on art and artist policy, as well as in decision-making related to the resourcing of the arts.

In this essay, I will reflect on the cultural phenomenon of artist residencies from two perspectives that intersect in occasionally surprising ways. First as a potential form of cultural diplomacy, and second as an open platform for the honing of skills, primarily those specific to artistic professions.

I regard artist residencies as offering potential for combining an experience of slowness, long-term engagement in cultural groundwork, and non-visibility, which is not the same thing as invisibility. By 'non-visibility' I mean temporary oblivion away from the spotlight. My discussion will focus specifically on Finland, and the following case examples mainly describe Finnish practices.

I believe that artist residencies have the potential to remind people of the true meaning of cultural sustainability. Artist residencies are rhizomes that transform invisible connections into tangible, interlinked semiotic chains. This is why, for artists, a residency is both a creative sanctuary and a one-stop skill-fuelling shop.

FROM CRISIS TO CRISIS

The outbreak of the coronavirus pandemic in the spring of 2020 necessitated a radical reappraisal of all the usual societal, social and cultural conventions observed in times of normalcy. Free movement ceased, and it became impossible for people to meet face to face without taking special precautions or risking illness and spread of the virus. The pandemic also had a direct and immediate impact on artist residencies, which inherently revolve around the idea of connecting with people in new situations and places.

Finland's residency organisers and funding institutions responded quickly, doing what they could to help artists reorganise their work plans through multiple channels and novel forms of funding such as 'home residencies'. The pandemic shifted the focus of everyone's existence from mobility to staying put in one place. Communication became reliant on hybrid remote technologies, and some organisers even experimented with what they called 'digital residencies'.

During the pandemic, localism gained new-found importance in people's lives. The pandemic also highlighted the problems associated with constant back-and-forth air travel, a subject that was already under critical scrutiny in the wake of the climate crisis. The increased popularity of slow travel is seeing travellers spending longer periods of time at their chosen destination, which significantly alters their perception of time, while also increasing their sensitivity to observing meaningfulness in their immediate surroundings. Many cultural practitioners have been roused to action by the increased prevalence of abnormal climate conditions and extreme weather events.

Russia's invasion of Ukraine in February 2022 confronted us with yet another perturbing new reality that upturned many established conventions and cultural values. The war exposed the limitations of political processes and the narrow avenues available for delivering concrete assistance to people in obvious distress. As we have seen many times before in the course of history, the war posed an acute and immediate threat particularly to many artists and cultural practitioners.

With traditional political structures proving themselves to be ill-equipped to combat the threat faced by artists, the pandemic gave new visibility to the cultural and political agency of art and the power of artist residency networks. Dissident cultural practitioners who deploy symbolic weapons and embrace the free expression that is an inalienable part of both art and democracy are typically among the vulnerable groups directly in the aggressor's line of fire.

Russia's invasion of Ukraine highlighted the importance of existing grassroots networks. The 'residency rhizome' showed immediate readiness to face the crisis and respond to the needs of vulnerable groups. Within only a few months, the Helsinki-based Artists at Risk organisation mobilised 500 residencies to host artists in exile, but there is still a dire shortage of artist asylums.[4] It bears noting that the threat not only affects artists in the invaded country, Ukraine, but also dissidents in the attacker country, Russia, and its ally Belarus, where artistic freedom is blocked in numerous ways and the freedom and lives of artists are equally at risk.[5]

War gives visibility to things that are often forgotten in peacetime. Outside times of crisis, preventive action tends to be forgotten and under-resourced. Political influence can be exercised pre-emptively through symbolic cultural actions, or what is traditionally called cultural diplomacy.

Cultural diplomacy can be defined as long-term, multi-level cultural relations through which nation-states consciously pursue goals of strategic national importance. It can also refer to cultural exchange or dialogue that transcends the narrow interests of the nation-state and more broadly supports the common good.[6] The definition commonly cited in current discourse is that coined by Milton C. Cummings, who describes cultural diplomacy as 'the exchange of ideas, information, values, systems, traditions, beliefs, and other aspects of culture, with the intention of fostering mutual understanding.'[7]

Cultural diplomacy is a topic that is conspicuous by its absence in current discourse on Finnish cultural policy and foreign policy. These days Finnish embassies play a less visible role as cultural envoys than they once did, and the Finnish Ministry for Foreign Affairs has even discontinued its cultural department. Over the past few decades, Finland's official avenues and funding schemes for international cultural relations have essentially focused purely on promoting cultural exports and international markets for Finnish creative industries.[8]

The Arts and Culture Barometer is an annual survey targeted at artists and cultural organisations based in Finland. The 2018 survey charted respondents' perceptions and experiences of mobility, both concerning art in general and their own work.[9] The survey was circulated widely within the arts community, especially among organisations that in some way support artist mobility.

The barometer identified a total of 215 Finnish organisations that are somehow involved in supporting the mobility of art and artists. Only 38 of these organisations responded to the survey, most of which are third-sector organisations and foundations. The most active international cultural networkers are Finland's cultural and scientific institutes, as well as information centres representing specific fields of the arts. All are relatively small associations or foundations with extremely limited resources, despite the government subsidies they receive.[10]

Roughly a quarter of the organisations that responded to the survey, i.e. fewer than ten respondents, were government agencies, embassies or consulates. From their point of view, fostering 'mobility' primarily meant promoting international work opportunities, facilitating commercial success, and building the national brand image.

In 2017, the average sum in mobility grants awarded by the respondent organisations was €20,000, indicating that the majority of funding organisations distribute very small grants at best. All the respondents emphasised that there is a growing need for funding, and that international contacts are on the rise.

Although many funding organisations emphasised the central importance of cultural diversity, equality and sustainability, this did not find reflection in their funding decisions and distributed grants. Their overriding goal was to facilitate the international networking of Finnish artists and thereby advance their professional development and employment opportunities.

5   https://artistsatrisk.org/?lang=en (accessed in February 2024).

6   Marita Muukkonen, 'Utifrån Ukrainakriget: Nya förutsättningar och utgångspunkter för samarbete med omvärlden', presentation at *Kultur i Almedalen* in Visby, Sweden, on 3 July 2022.

7   See Ang Ien, Yudhishthir Raj Isar and Phillip Mar, 'Cultural diplomacy: beyond the national interest?', *International Journal of Cultural Policy*, 21:4 (2015), pp. 365–81 and Sigrid Weigel, *Transnational foreign cultural policy – Beyond national culture: prerequisites and perspectives for the intersection of domestic and foreign policy* (Stuttgart: ifa, Institut für Auslandsbeziehungen, 2019).

8   See Milton C. Cummings, *Cultural Diplomacy and the United States Government: A Survey. Cultural Diplomacy Research Series* (Washington: Americans for the Arts, 2009).

9   www.okm.fi (accessed in February 2024).

10 See Maria Hirvi-Ijäs and Irmeli Kokko, 'Grounding Artistic Development', Taru Elfving, Pascal Gielen and Irmeli Kokko (eds), *Contemporary Artist Residencies: Reclaiming Time and Space* (Amsterdam: Valiz, 2019), pp. 87–101.

The above-mentioned *Arts and Culture Barometer* examined data from 2017–18. Recent global crises have undoubtedly impacted the work of many mobility-supporting organisations, but there is no reason to assume that their basic structures or funding base have changed substantially.

The Arts Promotion Centre Taike is a Finnish government agency whose website emphasises the importance of supporting artists who are directly impacted by Russia's war on Ukraine.[11] Taike's website mentions organisations involved in this effort, including the third-sector information centre Frame, the Artists at Risk organisation, and Artinres, a listing of Finnish artist residencies maintained by the Studio Foundation.

In 2015, the British Council commissioned a report on trends in cultural diplomacy, which revealed that the practical work of cultural diplomacy is effectively left to third-sector initiatives.[12] In many European countries there are of course public agencies involved in formal cultural relations, such as the British Council network.[13] In his conclusions the report's author, John Holden, lists the implications of this trend, pointing out that governments need to create conditions for broad and deep cultural exchange to flourish. He notes that they should also work together with commercial and third-sector initiatives, adopting a mix of strategies and embracing long-term relationship building. Holden furthermore emphasises the importance of cultural exchange and hospitality. Beyond just promoting cultural exports, governments should balance out instrumental goals by also fostering pluralism, cultural diversity and awareness of their significance.

11 https://instituutit.fi/ (accessed in February 2024). See also Sakarias Sokka, Vappu Renko and Emmi Lahtinen, *Toimialojen edistäjät ja toiveiden tynnyrit. Taiteen tiedotuskeskusten toiminta ja asema* (Helsinki: Cupore Centre for Cultural Policy Research, 2020).

12 https://www.taike.fi/fi/ukrainan-tilanne (accessed in September 2022)

13 John Holden, *Influence and Attraction Culture and the Race for Soft Power in the 21st Century* (London: British Council, 2015), p. 34.

14 Ibid.

It is also important for Finland to recognise the international potential of its diverse grassroots practitioners. The last thing anyone needs is state-controlled cultural propaganda or heavily instrumentalised cultural production.[14] Finland should therefore initiate discussion on the topic of cultural diplomacy in its various forms, while also taking a close look at the significance, efficacy and resourcing of its diverse existing international networks at various levels.

DEVELOPMENT OF ARTS PROFESSIONS AND SKILL MAINTENANCE

Artist residencies – which have historically evolved out of collegial networks – have come to play an important role in the overall development of art, artistic practices and art-related professions. This fact comes to light in the aforementioned *Arts and Culture Barometer* targeted at Finland's artist community, in which 82 % of the respondents regarded international artist residencies as being important, primarily for their personal artistic development. Almost 70 % of the respondents emphasised the importance of domestic residencies, although only about a tenth had applied for a domestic residency in 2017.

Peace and quiet to concentrate on artistic work is the primary positive feature of artist residencies as reported by the survey respondents. Another asset is the opportunity to connect with fellow artists, which the respondents regarded as significantly more valuable than networking with experts, institutions or other intermediaries. Collegial networking is generally regarded as more important than specific collaborative projects or work opportunities that might arise through a residency.

The respondents reported that they were keen to participate in residencies at various stages of their career, offering them an opportunity to reappraise their work from fresh perspectives at different waypoints on their artistic journey. Working in an inspiring new environment can moreover lead to new discoveries and wholly new directions in an artist's practice.

Both the annals of history and the feedback of artists-in-residence emphasise the importance of residencies as a place of growth and learning. Italian Renaissance academies are often described as the precursors of modern-day artist residencies – indeed many even today are still affiliated with art academies.[15] According to this reading of history, early art academies provided a forum for knowledge sharing, debate, discussion and innovation, thus fostering new artistic freedom and enabling artists to break away from the hierarchical, authoritarian grip of professional guilds.

This interpretation suggests a hierarchical division between artists as free creatives and artisans governed by the guild system, with independent creativity and originality of expression being deemed as holding higher value than convention-ruled anonymous craftsmanship.

In my opinion, artist residencies should not be built upon such a sharp division between artistic and artisanal forms of working and learning. Richard Sennett – an advocate of pragmatic philosophy, sociologist and former professional musician – regards professional identity and excellence as being strongly linked to 'joined skill in community', craftsmanship and social recognition.[16]

Analysing Italian goldsmiths' workshops during the early Renaissance, Sennett describes the guild system as a cradle of excellence and professionalism, with masters, journeymen and apprentices working side by side in the same workshop.[17] After seven years of basic training and gaining official apprenticeship qualification, journeymen would complete their education by travelling and working in different towns and workshops in the guild network. To qualify as a master, journeymen were expected to gain experience not only in their craft, but also in leadership, management of resources, work processes, the broader workings of the trade and society overall. The journeyman then returned to his own workshop equipped with a deeper understanding of his trade as well as new ways of thinking passed on by other professionals.

The guild system was essentially based on mobility, networking and learning through new experiences and encounters. But, because the guild hierarchy prescribed exactly what members were permitted to do with their skills, the strict structures became unsustainable in the wake of social change, and the whole guild system eventually fell apart.[18]

15 See Mia Huttunen, *Paha propaganda, hyvä kulttuuridiplomatia?* (Helsinki: Tutkijaliitto and the blog of the journal *Tiede & Edistys*, 5 September 2019).

16 Taru Elfving, Pascal Gielen and Irmeli Kokko (eds), op. cit., p.15.

17 See Richard **Sennett**, *The Craftsman* (New Haven: Yale University Press, 2008).

18 Ibid., p. 53 ff.

Artists receive professional and social recognition not only for their technical skills, but also for the pursuit of originality and fresh creative insight. Whereas artisans dedicate themselves to polished craftsmanship, free artists have traditionally embraced innovation and a more spontaneous creative process. For free artists, creative autonomy has always been paramount – at least as far as allowed by demanding clients, patrons, conventions or other social controls.

One of the central questions addressed by art academies concerns the professional skills required in order for someone to qualify as an artist. Indeed, equipping artists with professional skills is every art academy's core mission. International networking is today regarded as a core part of artistic competence by Finland's highest institution of art education, the Academy of Fine Arts (Uniarts Helsinki). Special foundation-funded programmes targeted especially at alumni have been set up to enable artists to work in residencies.[19]

Based on interview material collected from alumni of the Academy of Fine Arts, many artists find that completing a residency shortly after graduation can be a particularly eye-opening experience that can have a major formative influence on the future direction of an artist's work.[20] Working side by side as equals with a diverse group of colleagues of varied ages, cultural backgrounds, and career stages offers a unique opportunity for cross-fertilisation and knowledge exchange.

The combination of flexibility and multiculturalism offered by an international artist residency provides fruitful soil for artistic growth. The temporary sense of community instilled by a residency can also benefit artists at later stages in their career. By working outside their normal conditions, artists not only learn new things but invariably also unlearn old views and habits. In an international residency, artists work side by side with colleagues from different backgrounds, which brings to light the differing realities of practicing art in other parts of the world. For many, a residency is an extremely valuable opportunity for exchanging information, learning, and communicating with colleagues as equals.

19 Ibid., p. 80.

20 https://www.uniarts.fi/projektit/kuva-taiteen-kansain-valiset-verkostot/ (accessed in February 2024).

Concerns related to time, money and cultural rights are an inescapable part of every artist's reality. The artist residency network is integrally connected to wider processes of cultural, political and economic change, and the evolution of the profession is itself a political issue that warrants addressing in cultural negotiations.

Artist residencies are often seen as offering an alternative to institutionalised and commercial market structures, particularly as they operate on the founding principle of open, inherently non-profit-driven work processes. They are perceived as safe havens for autonomous creative growth for all artists needing it. Even so, residency networks have their own in-built economic structures, through which they effectively form a labour and art market in their own right.[21] Artist residencies are not entirely free of hierarchies, much as they may be founded on the principle of autonomy from the commercial art market and the authoritarian tradition of the guild system.

A residency can thus teach valuable lessons pertaining to power structures, competition and other professional realities of working as an artist. Interviews suggest that there is wide variation in how artists respond to competition, and this depends greatly on the individual. It is important for the artist to be confident in their professional identity and artistic goals, and they must be conscious of the implications of their professional choices in the vicissitudinous realities of the artworld.

Diversity, open structures and adaptability are among the documented assets of artist residencies, as evidenced by artist feedback and analysis carried out within the residency network. Another key strength is that a sufficiently large number of residencies have successfully maintained autonomy from the institutionalised art world and they have kept finding innovative ways of organizing and renewing themselves.[22]

The experience and knowledge that is gathered in artist residencies could be used more effectively as a tool for driving learning and development of art professions. I believe it would be fruitful to engage in a deeper study of artist residencies as a medium of signification. Added to that, knowledge derived from residency networks could be utilised to raise awareness of the importance of cultural values and cultural diversity.[23]

CULTURAL SUSTAINABILITY

In Finland, artist residencies are linked both to cultural policy and education policy, but at the moment, they occupy the margins rather than the core. I believe that artist residencies should be viewed as an integral part of wider sustainability policy, especially considering cultural sustainability. Mobilising residencies to accept artists in crisis could thus be regarded as an aspect of national emergency policy, with renewable cultural competence being recognised as a core aspect of sustainable development.

Artist residencies are continually expanding their mycelial networks. The mycelium metaphor aptly illustrates the idea of a non-hierarchical organisation in which there are multiple entry and exit points and no need for a definitive outcome or chronology. The mycelium is fundamentally a non-visible entity that eschews a final 'result' and evades quantification of its efficacy. In the same way as botanical organisms store energy in their subterranean horizontal rhizomes, it is important that we nurture the energy, invisible expertise and wellspring of fresh thought that resides in collective cultural initiatives. These rhizomes must be kept nourished for the future.

21 Maria Hirvi-Ijäs and Irmeli Kokko, op. cit., p. 91.

22 Livia Alexander and Natalie Anglès, 'Embedding/ Embedded… A Residency Perspective from New York', Taru Elfving, Pascal Gielen and Irmeli Kokko (eds), *Contemporary Artist Residencies: Reclaiming Time and Space* (Amsterdam: Valiz, 2019), p. 174.

23 Francisco Guevara, 'Challenging the Sense of Time and Space: An Ethical Confrontation in Artist Residencies', Taru Elfving, Pascal Gielen and Irmeli Kokko (eds), *Contemporary Artist Residencies. Reclaiming Time and Space* (Amsterdam: Valiz, 2019), p. 134 ff.

24 Maria Hirvi-Ijäs and Irmeli Kokko, op. cit., pp. 90–91.

Hedge bindweed was added to the national list of harmful invasive alien species in 2012. It has been thought to grow natively in the shrubbery, grasslands and seaweed mounds of the archipelagos and southern coast. However, doubt has recently been cast on this, and it was more likely introduced to Finland, possibly already in the eighteenth century. The first reference to it in the literature is from 1754. The Royal Academy of Turku is thought to have distributed the plant in the 1750s and 60s. Hedge bindweed is held to be native to Seili and has not been eradicated.

Kalle
Hamm

Untitled

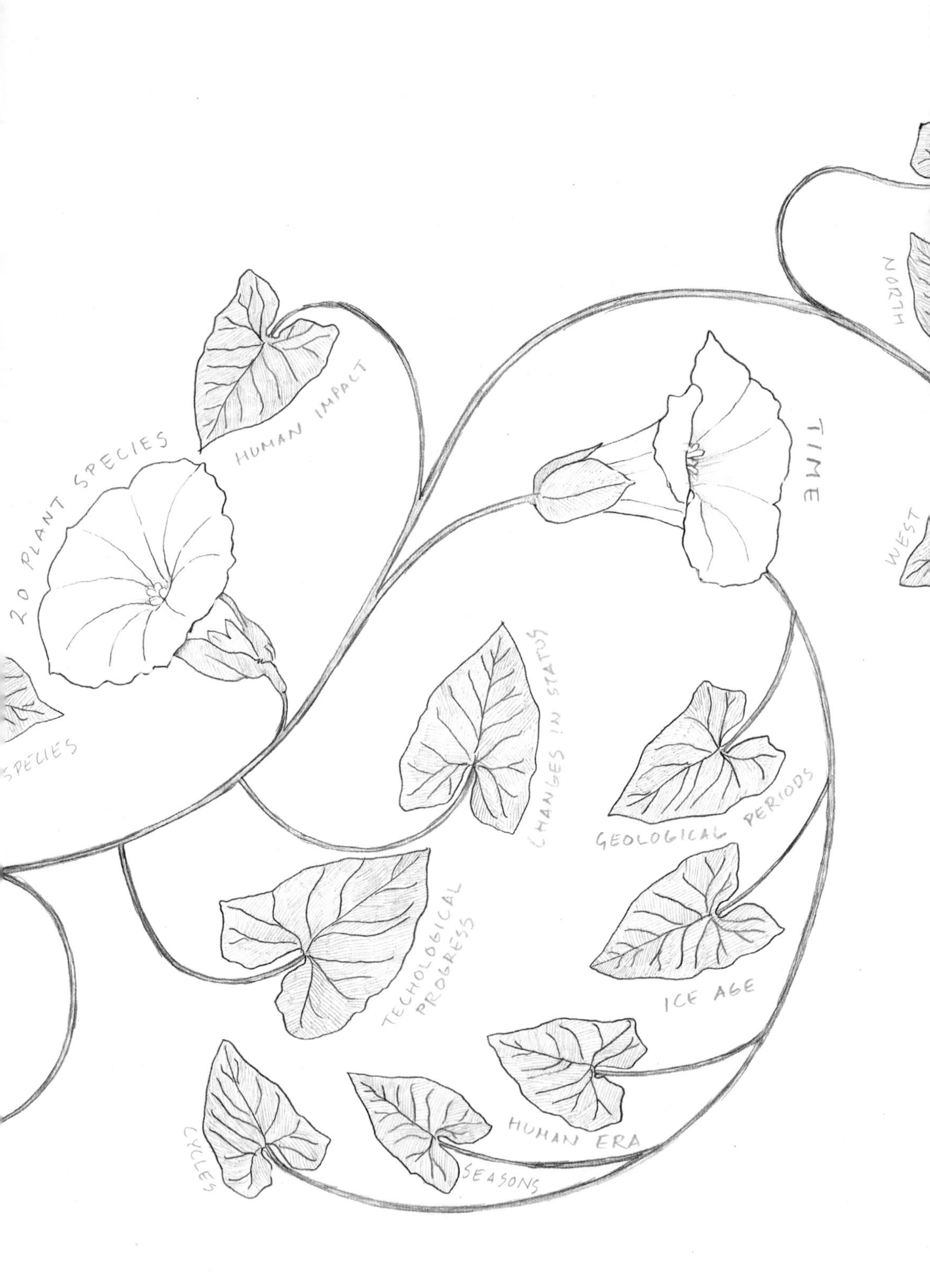

20 PLANT SPECIES
HUMAN IMPACT
SPECIES
TIME
NORTH
WEST
CHANGES IN STATUS
GEOLOGICAL PERIODS
TECHOLOGICAL PROGRESS
ICE AGE
HUMAN ERA
CYCLES
SEASONS

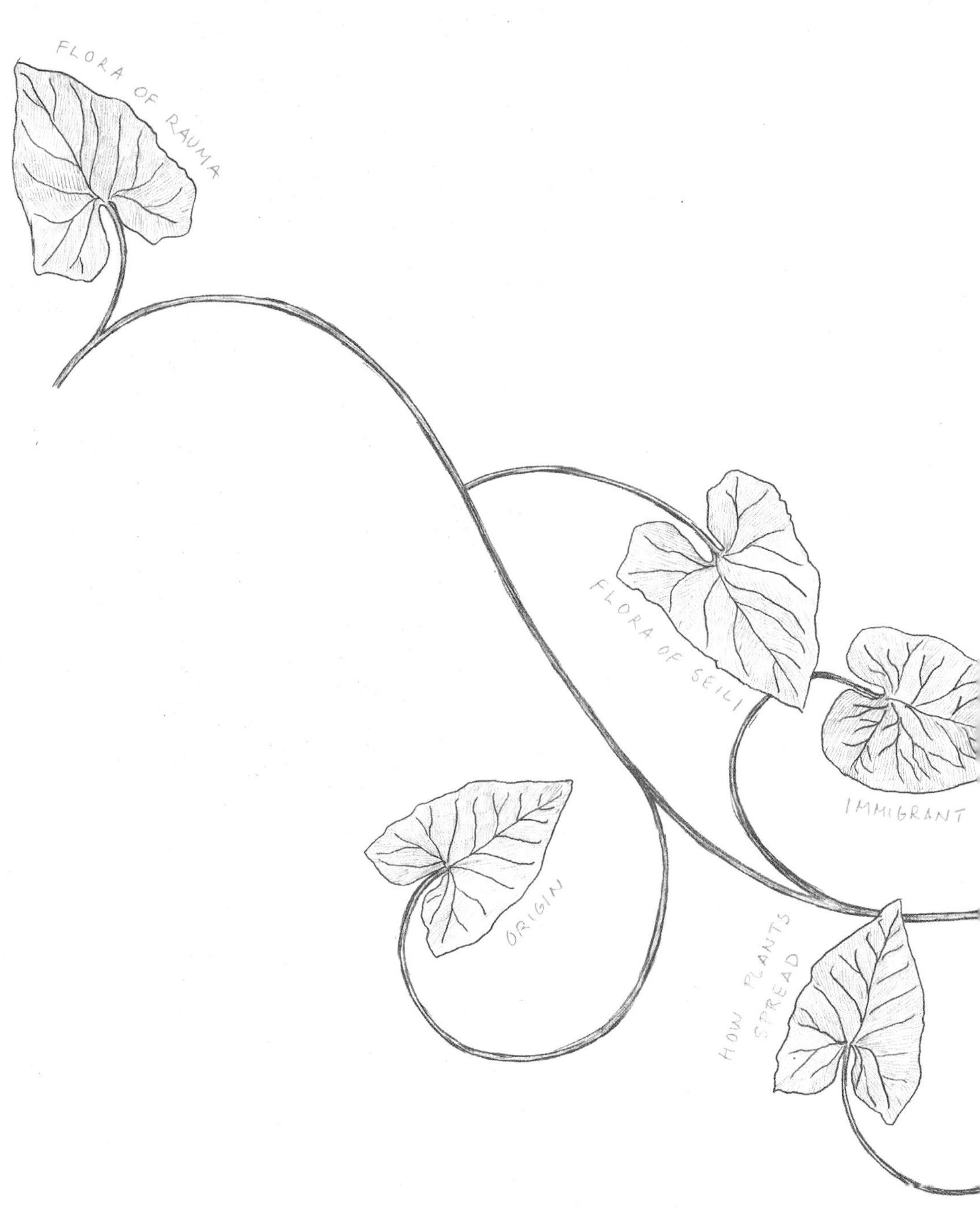

FLORA OF RAUMA
FLORA OF SEILI
IMMIGRANT
ORIGIN
HOW PLANTS SPREAD

Kalle Hamm (1969) is a visual artist based in Helsinki. His socially and politically engaged work often examines the importance of plants as raw materials and sustainers of life on Earth. Since 1998 Hamm has collaborated with Dzamil Kamanger, a Kurdish artist from Iran. The two artists have created conceptual gardens introducing viewers to the global cultural history of plants. In 2015 they founded the Band of Weeds sound collective to address the surrounding world from the point of view of plants, but within the limits of what is humanly possible.

During the pandemic Band of Weeds focused on the project *The New Pangaea,* a body of work examining the interaction of humans and plants on the Island of Seili in Finland. It has been realised within the CAA (Contemporary Art Archipelago) project, in cooperation with the Archipelago Research Institute of the University of Turku. Hamm has also participated in dozens of solo and group exhibitions in Finland and internationally.

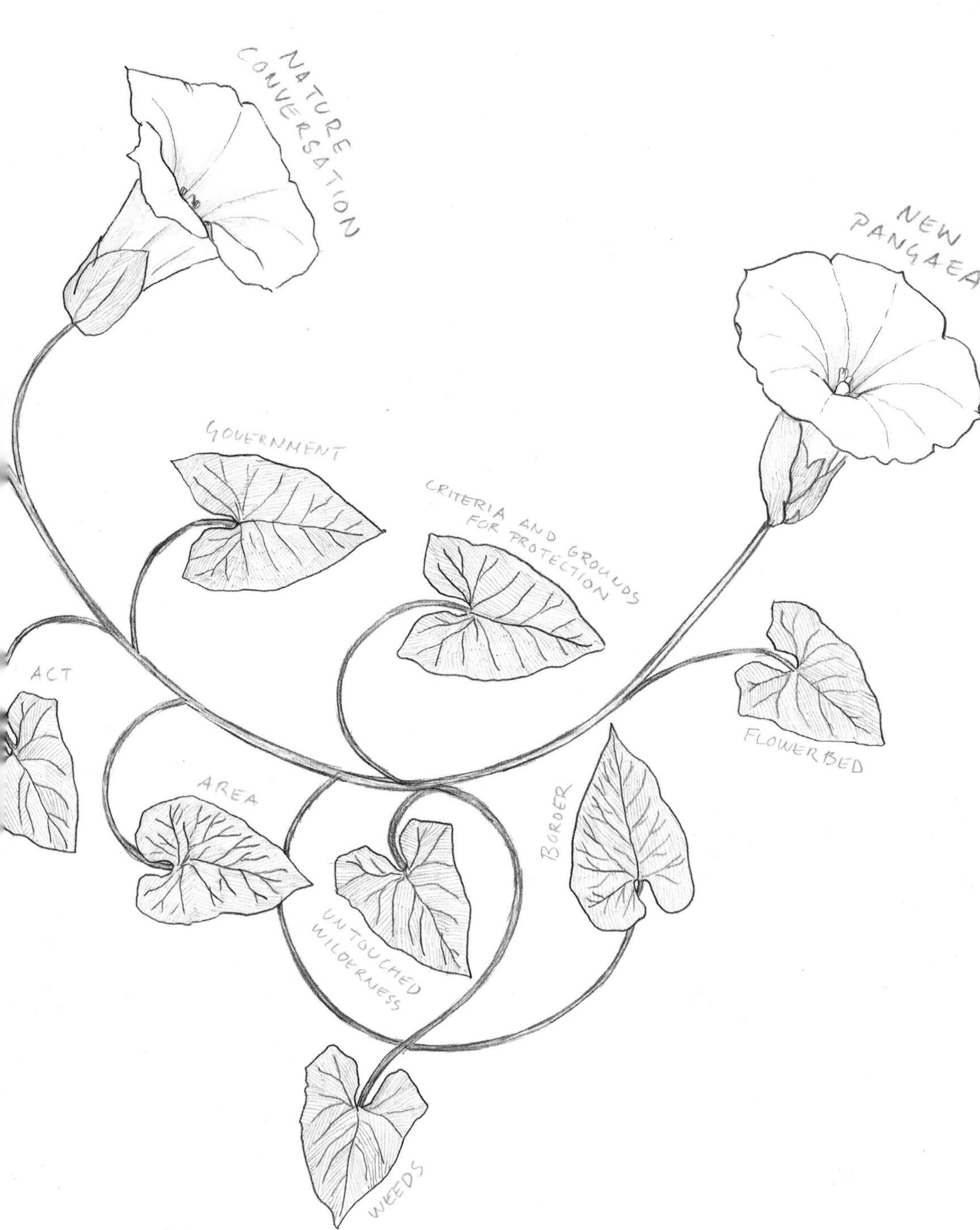

NATURE CONVERSATION
NEW PANGAEA
GOVERNMENT
CRITERIA AND GROUNDS FOR PROTECTION
ACT
AREA
UNTOUCHED WILDERNESS
BORDER
FLOWER BED
WEEDS

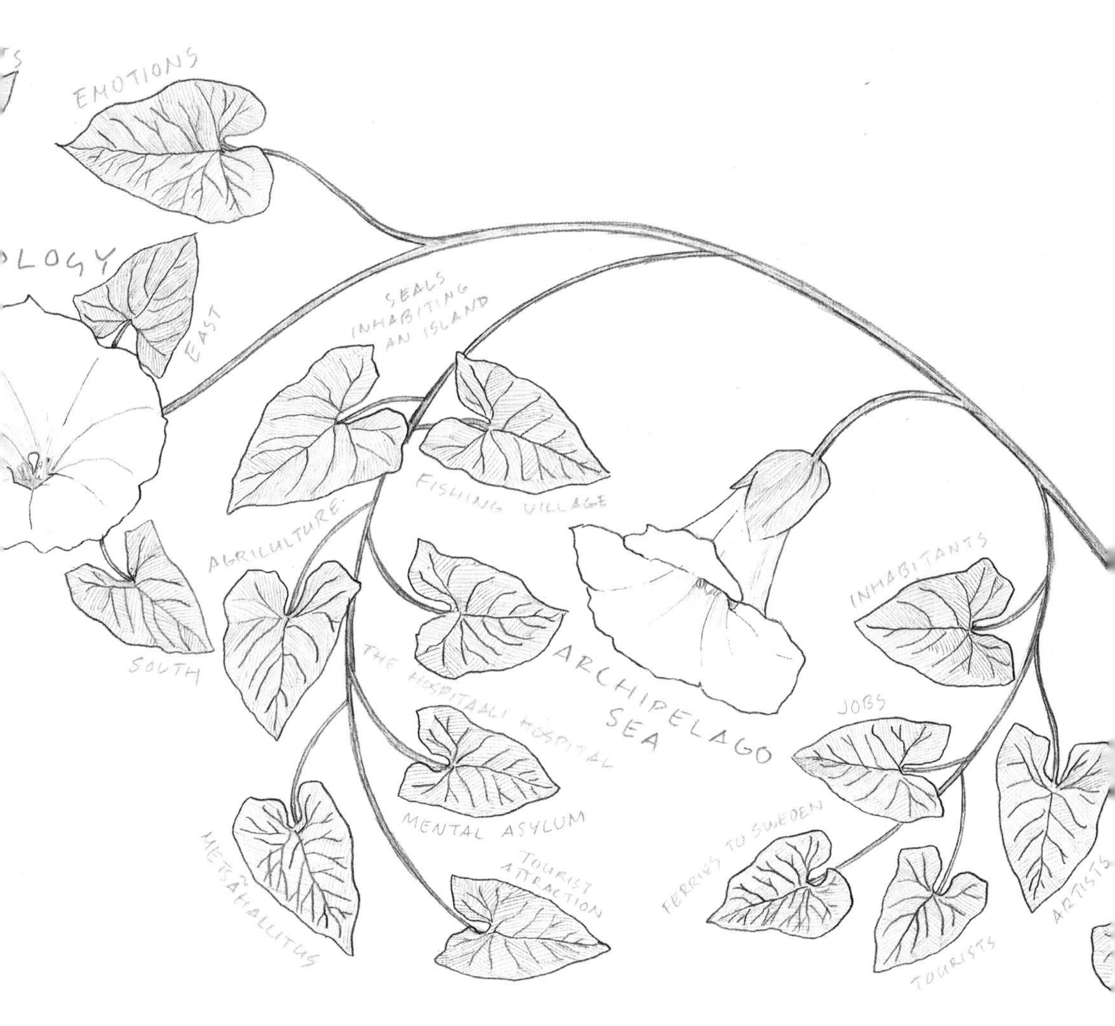
EMOTIONS
OLOGY
EAST
SEALS INHABITING AN ISLAND
AGRICULTURE
FISHING VILLAGE
SOUTH
THE HOSPITAALI HOSPITAL
ARCHIPELAGO SEA
INHABITANTS
JOBS
METSÄHALLITUS
MENTAL ASYLUM
TOURIST ATTRACTION
FERRIES TO SWEDEN
TOURISTS
ARTISTS

84

Residency as Field Work

Taru Elfving

Taru Elfving is a curator and writer based in Helsinki. She focuses on nurturing undisciplinary and site-sensitive enquiries at the intersections of ecological, feminist and decolonial practices. As Artistic Director of CAA Contemporary Art Archipelago she currently leads a research residency programme on the Finnish island of Seili in the Baltic Sea. Recent curatorial projects include 'Research Pavilion' (Uniarts, Helsinki, 2023), 'Hours, Years, Aeons' (Finnish Pavilion, Venice Biennale, 2015), 'Frontiers in Retreat' (HIAP, Helsinki, 2013–18) and 'Towards a Future Present' (LIAF, Lofoten, Norway, 2008). Elfving's co-edited publications include *Contemporary Artist Residencies: Reclaiming Time and Space* with Pascal Gielen and Irmeli Kokko (Amsterdam: Valiz 2019) and *Altern Ecologies* (Helsinki: Frame 2016).

1 Hamm has initiated and realised many of these works in collaboration with the artist Dzamil Kamanger.

2 The title of the work refers to Pangaea, the ancient supercontinent in which all today's continents were fused together.

In 2021 there was no spring. Or that is how it felt, when the persistently cool weather abruptly turned into a heat wave in May. The island of Seili burst into full bloom as the early summer blossoms appeared and disappeared. Spring was fast forwarded into full summer in a matter of days. I for one, alongside the artist Kalle Hamm, missed the spring on the island completely. Although Hamm had carefully planned the timing of his residency, the plants he came to document changed their annual schedule due to the unexpected temperature hike. Daisy, sea milkwort and red elderberry seem to have swiftly reacted to the heat, while we were not so agile with our plans. This meant another year of waiting and yet another return to the island.

Working with living plants in their own habitat requires adaptation to their seasonal and daily cycles in all their weather-dependent variations and climate upheavals. Hamm is no stranger to these demands, having worked with plants since 2005.[1] Yet our collaboration in Seili allowed him to commit to following these cycles for a number of years (2018–22), which brought into focus both the potential and the demands of artistic fieldwork engaged with and embedded within a complex ecosystem. Moreover, Hamm's experience and the process of making the body of work *The New Pangaea*[2] allows for insight into the promises and challenges of artist residencies in nurturing meaningful engagements with living organisms and environments.

Hamm presents his working process in this book in the form of a drawing. I approach it as a co-traveller, from a viewpoint that could be described as that of an entangled observer. My own practice as curator of the research residency programme *Spectres in Change* has been deeply transformative. I have been drawn into a relation with the island that has demanded repeated returns, rethinking and repositioning, while the intricate natural/cultural layers of change have been gradually revealing themselves, together with something about myself, with each return. Seili has demanded reckoning and adjusting to the diverse temporalities co-existing and clashing on the island: the cycles of plants and the sea, scientific fieldwork, accelerating tourism. With each return, the ruptures and irregularities have been felt with increasing intensity.

The residencies and collective retreats in Seili aimed at allowing for pausing or slowing down, for momentary withdrawals from the relentless pace and pressures of production. As participants we could take time to critically reflect on the sustainability of our practices, their methods and support structures. These pauses and withdrawals were unavoidably implicated in various other temporalities of change on the island. We also became part of the visitor economy. In addition to the unavoidable emissions of travel to the island, however carefully we treaded every step along the animal paths or the newly established nature trails left an ecological footprint.

Thanks to our recurrent visits over many years, we gradually became aware of our own implication in the transformations we were witnessing around us. Our questions were also being altered. What processes and rhythms of change are we part of here, as visitors, researchers, curators or artists? How do our practices align with, contribute to or resist the different yet interwoven tempos co-inhabiting and giving shape to the island? How to travel and reside in these times?

In this essay I attempt to follow and think with Hamm's drawing of the hedge bindweed. In its crawling, climbing, diverging and multiplying path across the pages, it guides my thoughts on residencies and suggests wordings to the questions emerging out of the multi-year collaborations on the island of Seili. Opening up towards wider concerns related to artist residencies, my essay reflects on Hamm's working process together with the sound collective Band of Weeds in Seili, which has so far produced a rich body of work across different media.[3] The work was realised as part of *Spectres in Change* by CAA Contemporary Art Archipelago in collaboration with the Archipelago Research Institute.[4]

WEEDS

The plant that Hamm chose for his drawing, as the representative for his working process in Seili, is the hedge bindweed (*Calystegia sepium*). Like many so-called common weeds, it is known by a range of different vernacular names, which stand as reminders of its lively shared history with humans: bearbind, bugle vine, heavenly trumpets, bellbind, hedge convolvulus, hooded bindweed, old man's nightcap, wild morning glory, bride's gown, wedlock, white witches hat, belle of the ball, devil's guts, hedgebell, granny-pop-out-of-bed. Wikipedia tells me it is a toxic weed with 'subcosmopolitan distribution throughout temperate regions'.[5]

Hamm's herbarium book describes the plant like this: 'Hedge bindweed was added to the national list of harmful invasive alien species in 2012. It has been thought to grow natively in the shrubbery, grasslands and seaweed mounds of the archipelagos and southern coast. However, doubt has recently been cast on this, and it was more likely introduced to Finland, possibly already in the eighteenth century. The first reference to it in the literature is from 1754. The Royal Academy of Turku is thought to have distributed the plant in the 1750s and 60s. Hedge bindweed is held to be native to Seili and has not been eradicated.'[6]

3 The members of Band of Weeds are Olli Aarni, Lauri Ainala, Kalle Hamm, Hermanni Keko, Anniina Saksa. The *New Pangaea* body of work consists, to date, of a sound work, performances, drawings, videos and a herbarium publication.

4 The project *Spectres in Change* was made possible by core funding from the Kone Foundation and additional support from the Swedish Cultural Foundation in Finland, the Arts Promotion Centre Finland and the Oskar Öflund Foundation.

5 https://en.wikipedia.org/wiki/Calystegia_sepium (accessed in February 2024).

6 See Kalle Hamm, *Uusi Pangaia: Kasvimatkoja Seilin saarelle* (Helsinki: CAA, 2023).

Hedge bindweed is one of numerous plants that have been intentionally distributed across the planet thanks to its decorative blooms and adaptation to a range of environments. With a near cosmopolitan presence across the Northern and Southern Hemispheres, it is today going through a change of status. Noxious weed or beautiful bloom, invasive alien or endemic, its uncertain status varies as the case of Seili reveals.

In Finnish the plant is popularly called 'thread of life' (*elämänlanka*). This vividly captures the essence of Hamm's project in Seili, where he has studied the island's plants with a focus on their history of migrations to and from the island, as well as the plants' interactions with humans since their arrival. What binds plants, humans and the island together? The island is young and continues to emerge out of the Baltic sea-in-formation due to the gradual ongoing land rise (glacial rebound) since the retreat of the glaciers around 10,000 years ago at the end of the last Ice Age. There are myriad plants that arrived on these shores before humans, and numerous others that have been introduced and eradicated, both intentionally and accidentally, as human activities has impacted the island over the centuries.

How are we, contemporary human residents and visitors, to assess who and what belongs here? Some former weeds are highly protected these days as they are threatened with local extinction such as the field cow-wheat (*Melampyrum arvense*), the island's icon and conservation success story, which was most likely introduced to Seili together with agriculture. Others disappear without hardly anyone noticing, such as the mother-wort (*Leonurus cardiaca*). Why is something, at a certain place and point in time, considered a weed? After years of observing the flora of Seili, Hamm argues that nature conservation could be considered here as a form of gardening, as active management of 'wild flower beds', which in turn has been affected by trends and transitions in knowledge and methodologies. The history of plants in Seili is not only a story of a ceaselessly changing environment but also a local natural/cultural history of different strategies of expansion and movement of both plants and humans, and a narrative of shifting cultural practices and values. On this island, the *where* is inseparable from the *when*.

From the perspective of a human time scale, hedge bindweed's 300 years of residence on the island seems like a rather committed period of becoming rooted as part of the dynamically evolving ecosystem. But there is a multitude of radically different yet interacting temporal scales at play here. The geological time of the evolving young sea and the new land, steadily rising from the waves on these shores at the pace of half a metre in 100 years, today encounters the uncertainties and abrupt transformations brought by climate change. What is considered a natural succession of different species populating the island entangles with the impacts of centuries of human inhabitation, both permanent and seasonal: fishing and seal hunting, agriculture and forestry, leprosy colony and mental asylum, nature conservation and environmental research, tourism and artistic work.

Years of work on the island have not only allowed for revisits to the site, which has deepened understanding of these complex spatial and temporal layers. They have also prompted reconsideration of our own assumptions and approaches. How does an artist's work differ from other ways of residing in Seili? How does the mobility of artists resonate with the various tempos and modes of movement making their marks on the island?

TIMES

If I had to describe the working process with three words, they would be vine, swirl and time: Vine, because the work was progressing at times as if growing flat on the ground, at other times leaning on others, while constantly branching out and reaching towards the light. Swirl, because you never knew what was going to turn up next. Phenomena and concepts were entwined into a whirlwind of cross references and in the eye of this vortex I was trying to make sense of my position as the author. Time, because the multi-layered history of the island, since the Ice Age until today, has left behind sediments, which were only gradually revealed during numerous visits.[7]

7 Kalle Hamm's personal notebook, 2022.

Hamm's description of his working process in Seili sketches a picture with words, resonant with the drawing on the previous pages, of progress that is neither linear nor predetermined. Returns to the island, time and again, were never the same. Rather the revisits followed the logic of seasonal cycles spiced up with unexpected encounters, abrupt obstacles, serendipitous diversions and leaps of faith. Returns were a promise and a premise of the whole project *Spectres in Change*. The aim of the support structure built on a multi-year engagement was to reduce the pressures of efficiency so as to nurture wandering and wondering without predefined goals.

Moreover, Hamm's words emphasise the collaborative and interdependent nature of his enquiry. He was working on the island part of the time together with the other members of Band of Weeds and throughout the years in close dialogue with the scientists at the Archipelago Research Institute, especially the biologist Jasmin Inkinen. Hamm also took part in some of the retreats I organised on the island with other artists. The more-than-human inhabitants of Seili were undoubtedly essential in making the work possible as guides and, perhaps, co-authors of the evolving body of work.

In actual fact, the process throws into turmoil the very notion of authorship. In an ecosystem, there is no single unit with clear boundaries or agents independent of others. The field recordings that form the vibrant backbone of the body of work make audible the dynamically shifting flows of nutrients in the plants. The signals of the plants thus 'voice' complex interactions between the individual plant and its environment, the composition of the soil and the fluctuating weather conditions. The signal is always specific to the moment and the location, yet in its situatedness it is also rooted in the sediments that form the island. It resonates with the multitude of interdependent rhythms and scales of change. Has the 'voice' of the artist become similarly decentred and situated in the process?

Plants have acted as guides in Hamm's project across these rhythms and scales. Deeper engagement with these beings, which appear immobile and rooted in place, have allowed for attunement to the diverse temporalities of change taking place on and around the island. What is happening here and now cannot be understood without a 'tidalectic'[8] approach

8 Elizabeth DeLoughrey, Elizabeth, *Allegories of the Anthropocene* (Durham, NC: Duke University Press, 2019), p. 2.

9 See also *Själö Poeisis* by the artist Lotta Petronella, a multidisciplinary collaborative work focused on the plants of Seili.

of zooming in and out, weaving connections between intimately close entanglements and planetary perspectives. Where and when of a place cannot be fathomed in isolation.

Plants have also acted as mediators between the elements of land, water and air. They draw attention to the shifting shorelines and other uncertain, porous boundaries with the myriad ways their life cycles crisscross these demarcations. In and through Hamm's work plants have allowed for the unearthing of stories that remain otherwise untold and undocumented.[9] They form a choir of plural perspectives on the entwined natural/cultural histories of migration, while making sensible the presences and interdependencies that otherwise remain intangible and unacknowledged. Working against 'plant blindness', Hamm's work has set out to draw forth plants from the backgrounds and shadows of attention. Yet in this process the involved plants and humans are also drawn into a novel relation that, perhaps, marks the beginnings of a deepening relationship of reciprocal care.

FIELDS

Perhaps the most 'eureka' moment experienced while working with Seili was the realisation that we, Band of Weeds, don't have to use live plants in our concerts, but that we can use recordings made in the field. We had previously considered that the live plants were part of the band as physical performers. However, the fact that Seili is a nature reserve and national heritage site, where transplanting plants is not permitted, encouraged us to modify our methods and to also reflect upon the ethical aspects of displacing plants: it raised the question of whether transplanting any plant is ethical in any context.[10]

10 Selina Oakes, 'Post-Residency Interview with artist Kalle Hamm', https://contemporary-artarchipelago.org/publication/post-res-idency-interview-with-artist-kalle-hamm/ (accessed in February 2024).

Hamm's focus on the migrations of plants, with and without humans, has over the years raised increasingly complex ethical questions about the relationship between humans and plants. In Seili these dilemmas led to a significant shift in the artistic practice and methods of Hamm and the Band of Weeds. In my thinking about residencies this connects with the necessity to critically rethink how artists (and curators or researchers) work. How is my practice positioned in this historical lineage of human–plant relations? How is it aligned with its various problematic aspects and legacies? How can it challenge unsustainable structures and values, and how can it encourage or experiment with other modes of relating?

Developing a deeper knowledge of a place or a plant takes time. Understanding a species in its ecosystem and its shared story with humans, requires attunement to its temporality. There are no shortcuts, just like scientific field research about environmental changes cannot be carried out without commitment to long-term, even cross-generational, processes of monitoring and observation. Similarly no place is an island, even less so in these times of climate breakdown. There is an urgent need to share insights of situated, embedded and embodied knowledge, between here and elsewhere, in order to make sense of their complex interdependencies.

This can be seen to both underline the potential of artist residencies and pose challenges to them. How to allow for longer term engagement of repeated returns, while also addressing the ecological footprint of travel? How to nurture a kind of time travel that is not determined by, for example, the timelines of the organisation or the available project funding, but by the temporalities of the more-than-human communities you engage with? How to acknowledge and support the different needs of artistic fieldwork, where critical reconsideration and readjustments of the assumptions and approaches are an integral part of the working process? How can residencies act as mediators between these situated practices of fieldwork and between differing disciplinary perspectives that meet in the field?

As the artist Saara Ekström argues, 'it's almost necessary to grow mycelia, a kind of an organic attachment to the landscape, before you have anything to say about it, or before it gives you something. This is why long or repeated residencies are significant, such as on Seili'.[11] In Seili I myself have come to think of mobility in residencies not solely in terms of geographical or spatial movement, but increasingly as time travel. Whether understood as space or time travel, in however minute steps or extensive leaps, this mobility also has built into it shifts in practices and perspectives. Growing rhizomatic roots in one place is a transformative process, as is developing reciprocal relations with other beings. This can involve becoming undisciplined by the conventions of the field of practice and by individual habits. Artistic fieldwork can then be seen also to rework its own field and its understanding of this field in many senses of the term, while being affected by the field where the work is embedded together with a multitude of other actors.

11 Saskia Suominen, 'Interview with artist Saara Ekström', https://contemporaryartarchipelago. org/publication/interview-with-artist-saara-ekstrom/ (accessed in February 2024).

12 See Robin Wall Kim-
merer, *Braiding Sweet-
grass: Indigenous
Wisdom, Scientific
Knowledge and the
Teachings of Plants*
(Minneapolis: Universi-
ty of Minnesota Press,
2013) and Amitav
Ghosh, *The Nutmeg's
Curse: Parables for
a Planet in Crisis*
(University of Chicago
Press, 2021).

Residencies have a specific potential for nurturing undisciplinarity, I would argue. Most of the art world's
support structures are focused on production or presentation. Like artistic education, residencies are rare institutional frameworks, where the focus is chiefly in fostering
the processes of artistic practice itself. Yet art education
is often governed by disciplinary formation, whereas residencies offer time and space for artistic development and
also unlearning at different stages of an artist's career.
Delving into fieldwork and cultivating the arts of noticing, for example by learning from plants as guides, might
well encourage this transition towards undisciplinarity.
Moreover, fieldwork and the related practices of attentive
long-term observation can rupture the atomised isolation of both individual disciplinary endeavours and spe-
cies-loneliness, while nurturing orientation to the world
as not solely an object or resource.[12]

ISLANDS AND ARCHIPELAGOS

The island has been not only a site, and certainly not merely
an object of study. Rather, it has acted as my co-curator in
this gradually unfolding work of nurturing undisciplinary and
site-sensitive enquiries in Seili. During the summer and autumn
of 2022, as we were sharing research methodologies (framed
as 'exercises in attentiveness') and presenting the first new artworks slowly emerging out of the years-long process, the medi-
ating role of the island was a visceral presence whether the
events took place in Seili or elsewhere. All the involved artists
had found their own ways of grounding, or landing, their practices on the island and had began growing tentative roots in the
rich soils of its natural/cultural sediments. These complex temporal and spatial sediments provided the shared foundations
for the different practices of sensing and making sense of the
transformations haunting both the island and our work there.

The island had guided and choreographed our work
during the past few years. Yet it can also be regarded as having
made the work possible in the first place. The geopolitical location of Seili along the historical maritime route between Sweden

and Finland, together with the post-glacial formation of the island with a natural harbour and ground suitable for agriculture and burials, made this an optimal site for a leprosy colony and a hospital in the seventeenth century. The available built infrastructure, connections and location led the Archipelago Research Institute of Turku University to be established here after the hospital was closed. And eventually the island made the ongoing work of CAA Contemporary Art Archipelago and artists possible.

In the case of Kalle Hamm and Band of Weeds, they had an initial project idea that was looking for a place. *The New Pangaea* was able to root itself in Seili, which then gave the project a distinct shape – much like specific environmental conditions of a habitat nurture certain plant species. The changing weather and seasonal shifts from year to year, as well as factors such as the impact of the global pandemic and the accelerating development of tourism, affected the work over the years, just like our dialogue with the researchers at the Institute. The artists' work, and also my practice as a curator, have been building on the legacies of all other previous institutions and human modes of inhabiting the island and navigating the surrounding archipelago. The biopolitical history of the island has demanded, time and again, that we pay critical attention to how our work is a continuation of particular genealogies of knowledge production with their inbuilt hierarchies, assumptions and blind spots.

13 Isabelle Stengers,
   'Introductory Notes
   on an Ecology of
   Practices', *Cultural
   Studies Review* 11(1)
   (2005), pp. 183–96.

Seili has called for sensitivity and responsiveness to its complex inheritances, so as to be able to adjust our practices in relation to it. If, as Isabelle Stengers argues[13], there is no practice independent of its surroundings, it is necessary to consider the processes and protocols through which we take our practices to new environments, bringing them into contact with different ecosystems and other fields of knowledge. Moreover, to be able to even begin to grow roots, we have had to figure out, first of all, how to land on this specific island. How do we arrive somewhere so rich in sediments of interconnected histories of landings that keep affecting the place? How have our everyday practices already made their mark on this very island? What do we bring with us, take away and leave behind?

Seili has guided us in our attempts to question presumptions of access – to the place, its largely unwritten histories, the intricate ecosystems in ceaseless transformation, or the knowledge and methods of scientists with decades-long embedded practices there. In the end, the island has challenged the idea that a residency can be granted by any organisation, or solely by humans to humans. The query into how to gain permission to land, or to gain temporary residence, has also led to questions concerning who and what is credited for making our work possible. How to pay gratitude to and acknowledge all that on this island has grounded, sustained and guided our enquiries? This essay is, alongside Hamm's drawing, part of the ongoing longer-term thinking and experimentation aiming at recognising and articulating the key roles the island has played in the processes of forming knowledge, understanding and unlearning.

While plants are classified from the human perspective as for example pioneers, weak competitors, weeds or endangered, the value-laden nature of these characterisations is sharply felt when applied outside of the scientific field and, especially, if projected back onto ourselves. Artist residencies, like bindweed, could be described as having a 'subcosmopolitan distribution across temperate regions' today. The title of Hamm's work *The New Pangaea* refers to a theory proposing that we have entered a new era, where the continents are reconnected again like in the ancient supercontinent Pangaea. But this time the distances between land masses are bridged by human mobility and the myriad intentional and accidental introductions, novel encounters and planetary feedback loops it has given rise to. Complex more-than-human co-dependencies and the far-reaching impact of our actions are undeniable at the moment, the era of The New Pangaea. How to reckon with our accountability and our shared, albeit unequally distributed, agency in this planetary archipelago?

They are constantly translating materials into new forms Ceramics become blankets, glass becomes puddles, and drawers become beds. In short, a truly malleable and material language. The flexibility in language resonates with mobility, as their projects – collaborative and individual – evolve in relation to space, both residential and mental.

Océane Bruel & dylan ray arnold

Last night years ago, passages and portals

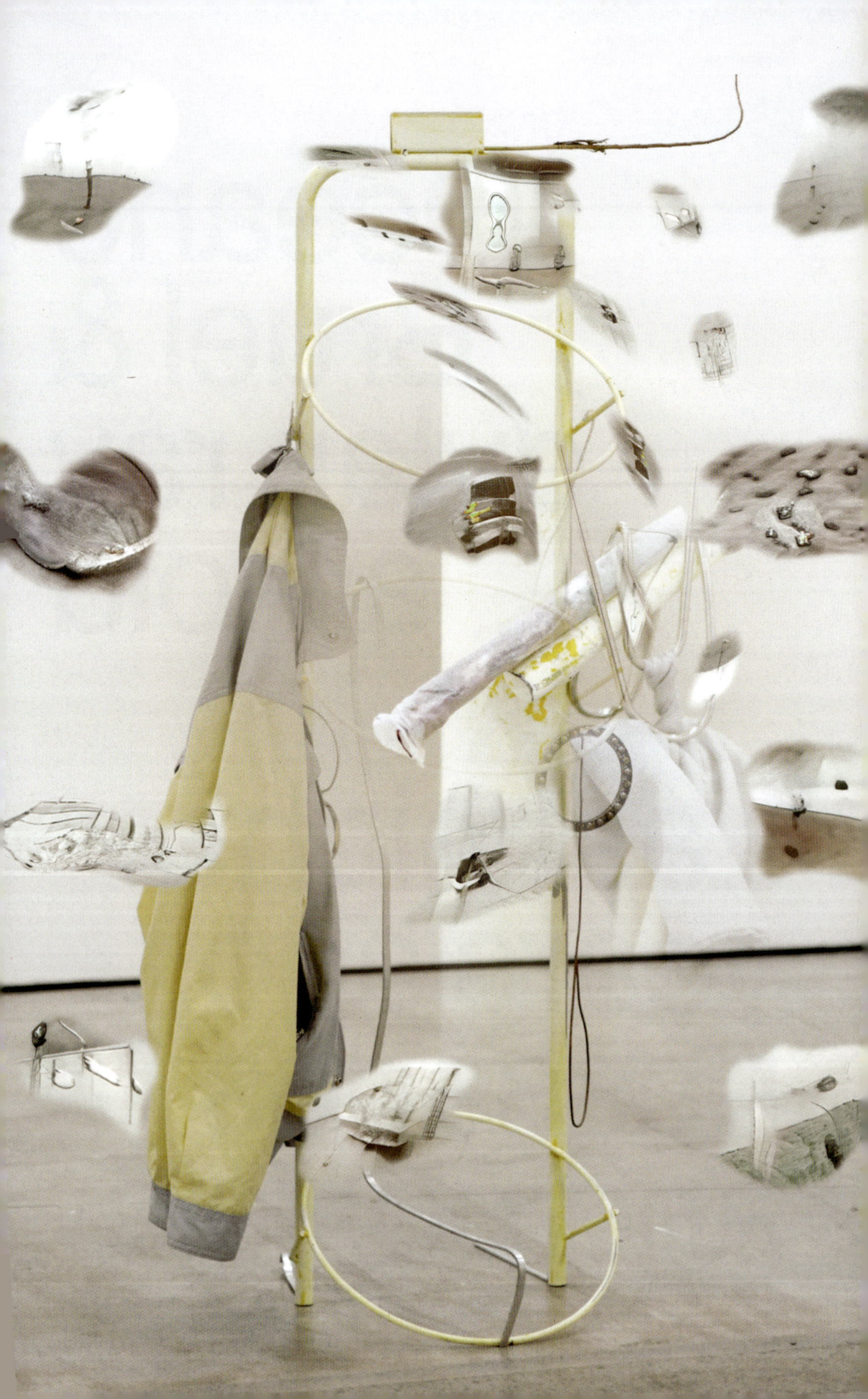

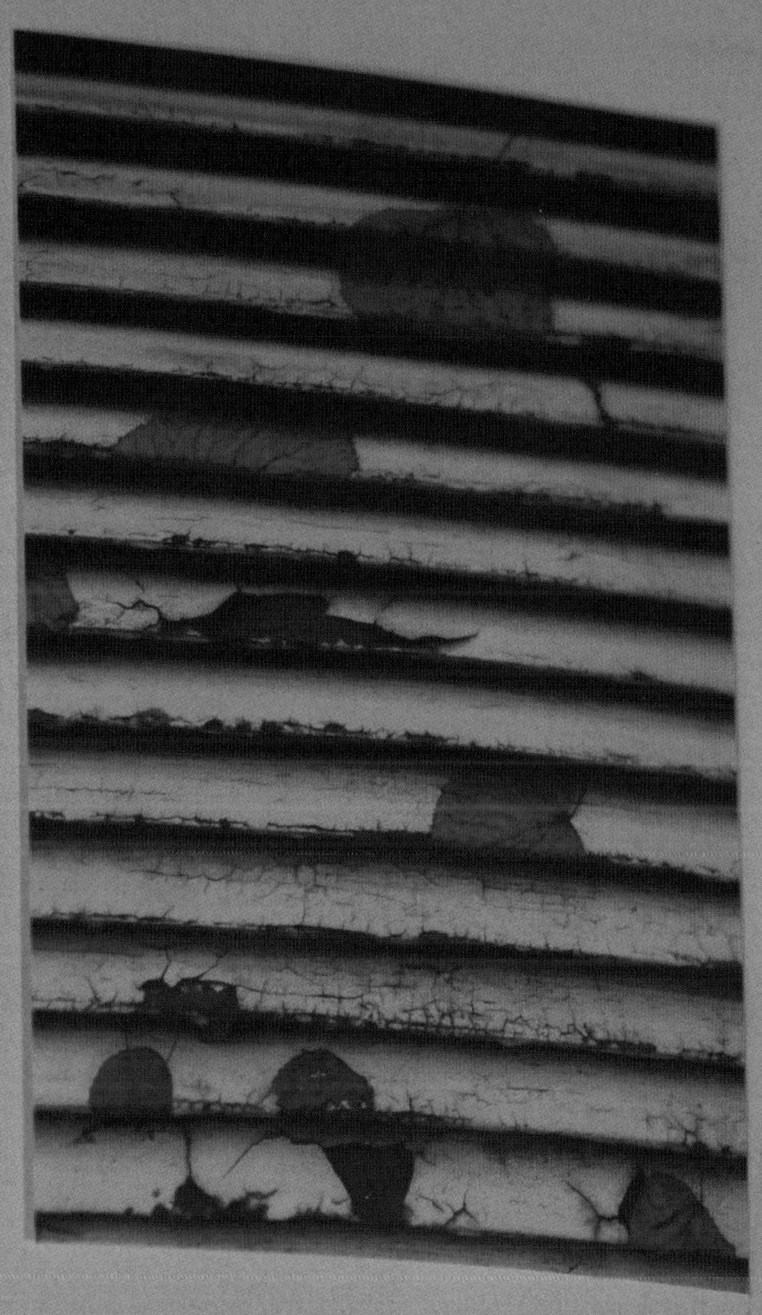

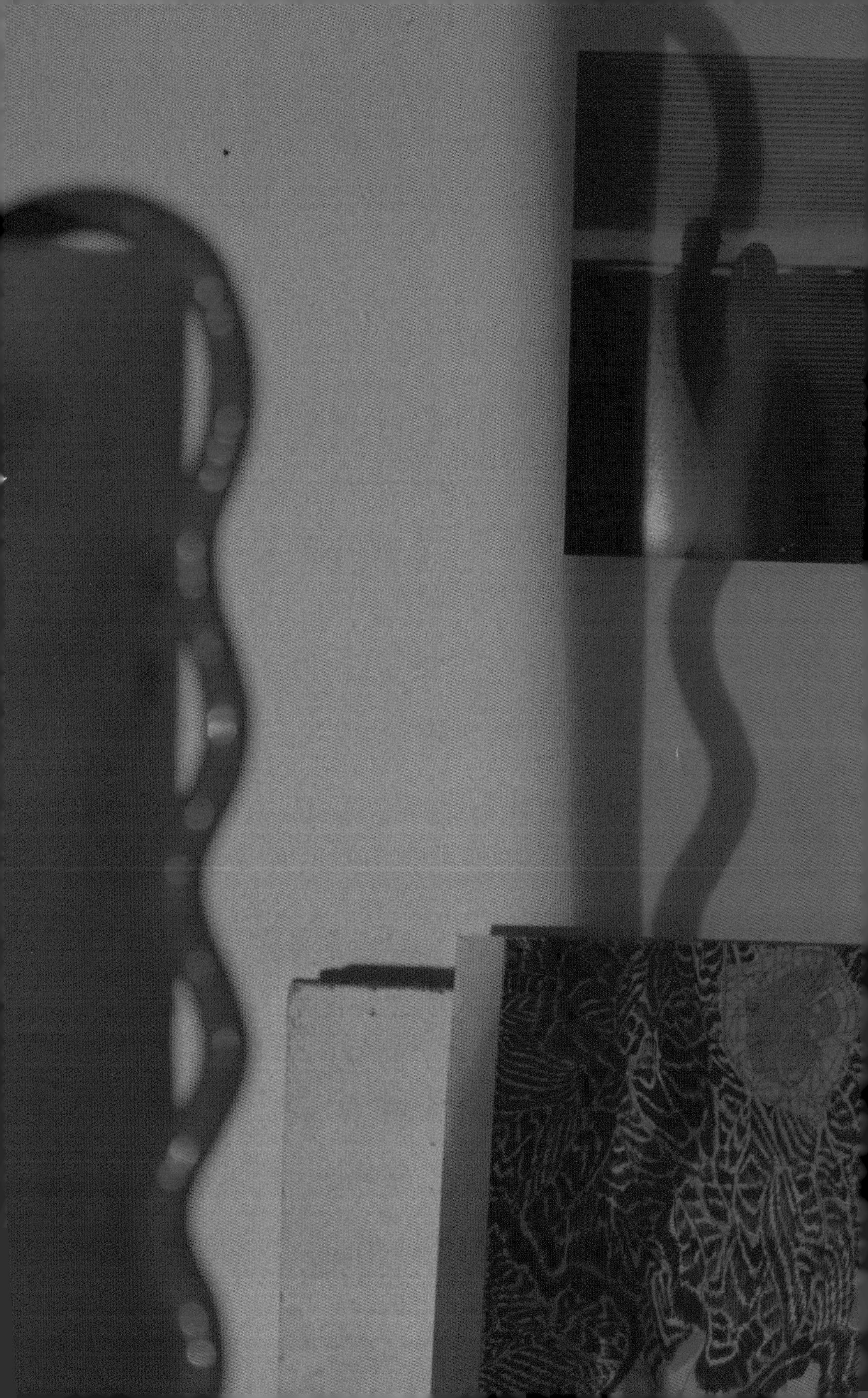

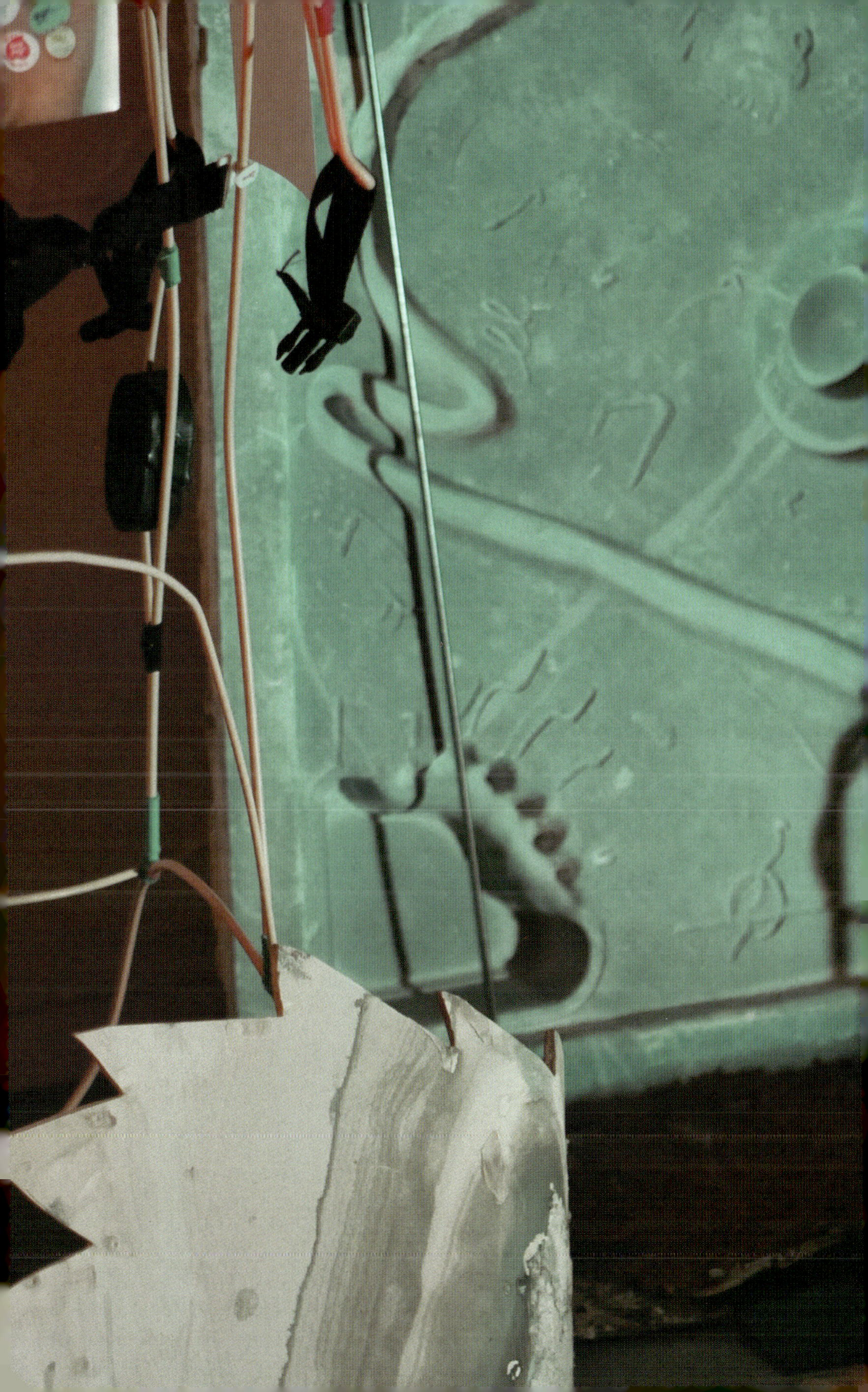

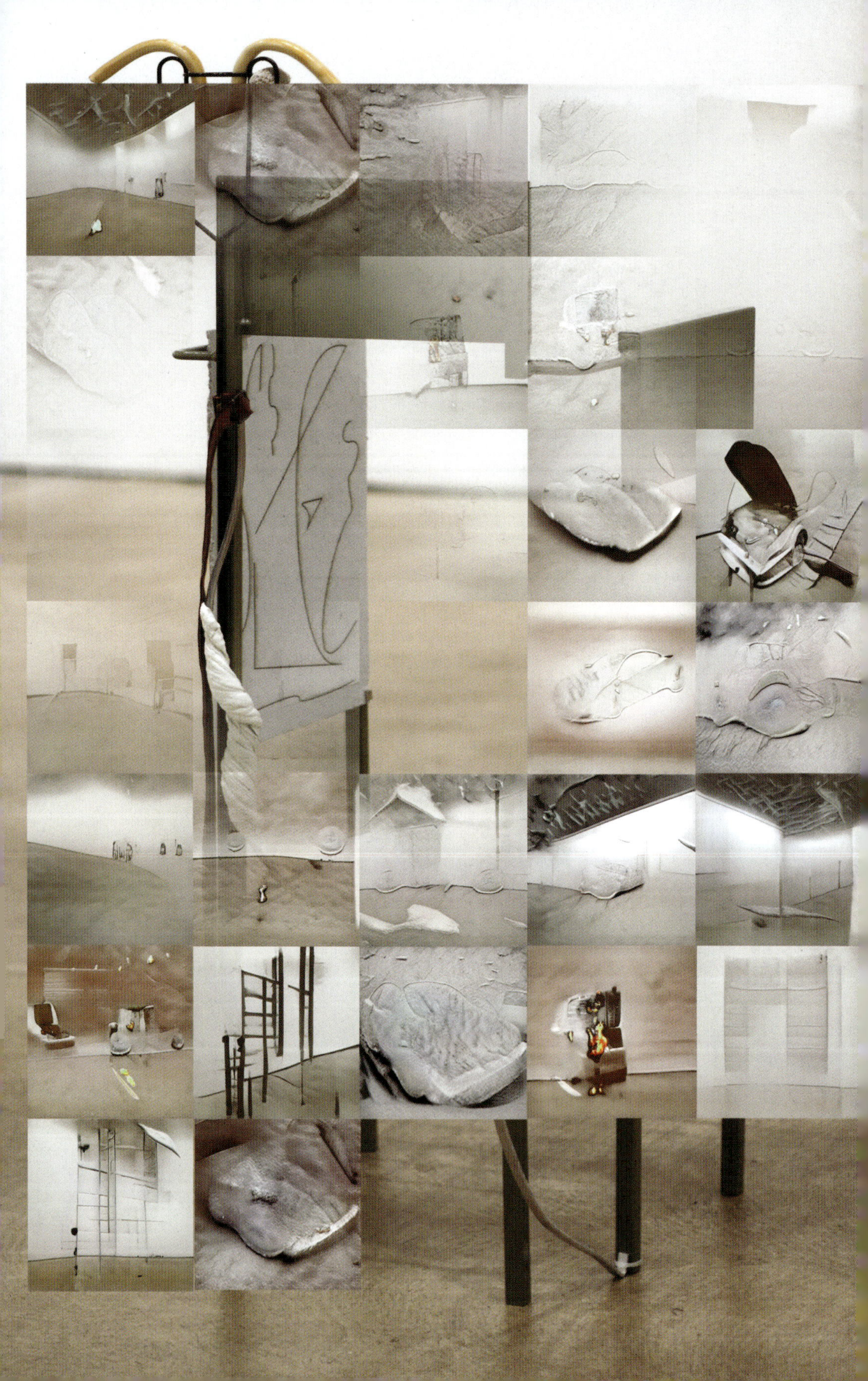

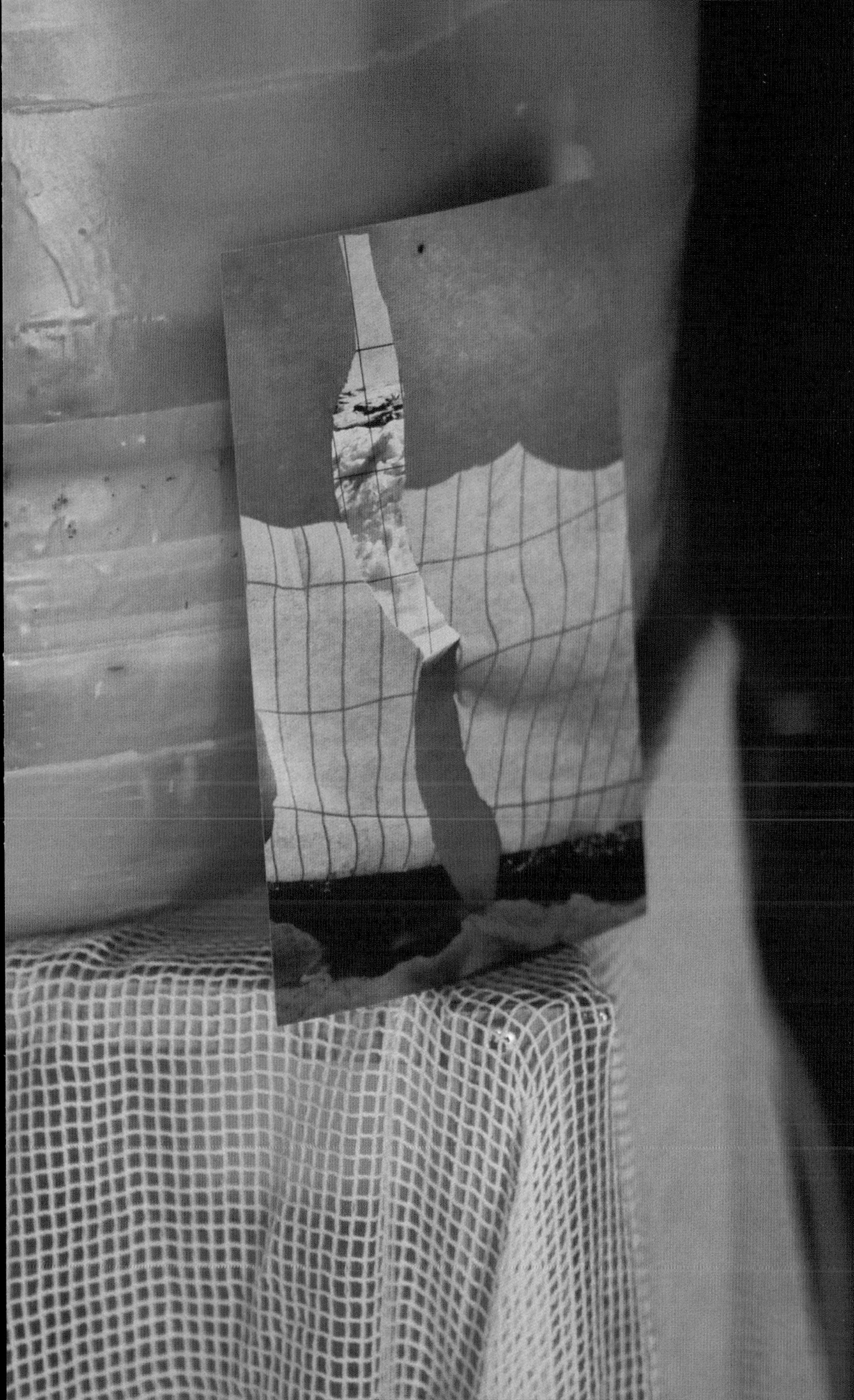

Océane Bruel (1991) is a French-born visual artist based in Helsinki. She holds an MFA from École Supérieure des Beaux Arts, Lyon. With its material-poetic and spatial approach, Bruel's work consists of sculptures, objects, and installations dealing with everyday environments, corporeality and affect. Her artistic work also includes the collaborative practice Touristes Tristes with dylan ray arnold. Bruel's work has been presented in group exhibitions internationally at Hobusepea Gallery, Tallinn, 2023, Salon am Moritzplatz, Berlin, 2021, Gether Contemporary, Copenhagen, 2020, Fondation Pernod Ricard, Paris, 2019 and elsewhere. Recent solo and duo exhibitions include 'hum' (Pengerkatu 7 Työhuone, Helsinki, 2022), 'L like Molecule' (La BF15, Lyon, 2020) and 'The Slow Business of Going' (HAM Gallery, Helsinki, 2020).

dylan ray arnold (1982) is a visual artist based in Helsinki. They hold an MFA from the Academy of Fine Arts, Uniarts, Helsinki. arnold works with sculpture, drawing, assemblage, installation and printed matter. They make psychedelic fabulations and spatial diagrams by playing with and manipulating quotidian materials, lines and spirits. Their artistic work also includes the collaborative practice Touristes Tristes with Océane Bruel. In addition to group exhibitions in the Nordic, Baltic Countries and France, arnold's work has been presented in solo and duo exhibitions in Finland such as 'Growth of Night Plants' (Forum Box, Helsinki, 2023), 'Frog and Toad's (Titanik Gallery, Turku, 2022), 'The Slow Business of Going' (HAM Gallery, Helsinki, 2020) and 'Nervous Systems' (Kunsthalle Turku, 2020).

Chewing, Folding, Articulating: On Océane Bruel's and dylan ray arnold's Material Languages

Katia Porro

Katia Porro is a US-born curator, writer and translator based in Clermont-Ferrand, France. She holds an MA in Contemporary Art and Curating from Sorbonne and an MA in the History of Design and Curatorial Studies from Parsons Paris – The New School. Porro is Artistic Director of In extenso in Clermont-Ferrand and Editor in Chief of the French contemporary art magazine *La Belle Revue*. She has held positions in various art institutions and galleries, such as the Amant Foundation in New York and Galerie Allen, Kadist and Palais de Tokyo in Paris, and she has curated exhibitions in France and abroad, for instance at Fondation Pernod Ricard, Doc ! and Treize in Paris, monopôle in Lyon and Gether Contemporary in Copenhagen. Porro has published texts in various publications, such as *Revue InSert*, *Revue 02*, *The Journal of Modern Craft*, *KLIMA* and *Disegno*.

1 Monique Wittig, *Lesbian Peoples: Material for a Dictionary* (London: Virago, 1980), p. 166.

Understanding a language without being able to speak it arouses a dizzying excitement. Using signs to concoct meaning, building your own vocabulary little by little, never truly understanding everything, but being able to perceive the essence of a thing, or of the thing you want to understand. This phenomenon has a name. Receptive multilingualism: the language constellation in which interlocutors use their respective mother tongue while speaking to one another, giving shape to new dialects that defy the laws of grammar and syntax while nonetheless remaining understandable to its speakers.

The artists Océane Bruel and dylan ray arnold have created a language from two others. In their constellation of dialects, words are replaced by objects and materials that defy the initial function to translate the poetic potential of things. In a work of speculative fiction about a land of lovers in the form of a dictionary, Monique Wittig wrote the following for the entry 'word':

Because of all the variations in meaning, shifts in meaning, losses of meaning that words may undergo, it happens that at a given moment they no longer operate upon reality or realities. Then they must be reactivated. This is not a simple operation and it may be accomplished in various ways. The most widespread is the one practised by the bearers of fables. Since the bearers of fables are constantly moving, they recount, among other things, the metamorphosis of words from one place to another. They themselves change the versions of these metamorphoses, not in order to further confuse the matter but because they record the changes. The result of these changes is an avoidance of fixed meanings. There also exists the tribute that the companion lovers pay for words. They constitute assemblies and together they read the dictionaries. They agree upon the words that they do not want to forgo.[1]

If 'word' were replaced by 'object' or 'materials' here, Océane Bruel and dylan ray arnold could be the bearers of fables. Although they both have their own individual practices, they have also been developing a collaborative practice together since 2014, working under the name Touristes Tristes and creating a dialect and identity distinct from its two differing origins – yet curiously similar. It is a dialect shaped by the artists' movements, their embrace of variation, their gestures that shift meanings, their avoidance of fixed meanings, their ode to metamorphoses, and agreements on what not to forgo. They are also companion lovers, since they form a couple, which allows for a fluidity and a sharing of the quotidian, space, rhythms, states of being and desires that shape their receptive multilingualism.

I met Océane Bruel and dylan ray arnold in 2019 while they were in residency at the Cité international des arts in Paris preparing their Touristes Tristes exhibition 'Be Sure to Collect All Your Longings and Let Me Crash On Your Shore'[2] that transformed elements of public transportation, the urban environment and travel to explore the idea of nomadic and carrier bodies. This introduction led me to understand how their collaboration reveals their shared perception of space and a shared way of making sense of the spaces they inhabit and traverse. Language, mobility, affect and a profound appreciation for how things and places shape our understanding of the world marked this first encounter and have continued to influence our exchanges, particularly as Océane is French and based in Helsinki, dylan is Finnish/Swiss and based in Helsinki, and I am American and based in France.

While I was preparing this text, my notes took on the form of various diagrams, not to depict the differences in each practice, but rather to visualise connections between them that are intrinsically spatial. Language has been the overriding theme. Touristes Tristes may feel like Océane's and dylan's common language, because they can't use their mother tongues for verbal communication between them, but also because they are constantly translating materials into new forms. Ceramics become blankets, glass becomes puddles, and drawers become beds. In short, a truly malleable and material language. The flexibility in language resonates with mobility, as their projects – collaborative and individual – evolve in relation to space, both residential and mental. These themes are accompanied by three prevailing gestures in this visualisation, serving as the common thread to my understanding of each practice within one larger constellation: chewing, articulating and folding.

Chewing appears in each of their practices in a both truly physical and symbolic manner. A press release for one of their collaborations attests to this. 'Taking their own anxieties, desires and fatigue as a point of departure, they chew ambivalent ideas, forms and materialities of contemporary mobility.'[3] The physical action of chewing is present in its traces. For Océane, it is in her use of peach pits, fortune cookie wrappers and artichoke petals (*Regarder les abeilles*, 2019; *Good Luck Your Way*, 2019). In dylan's work, puffed corn is bitten, chewed and stuck together in the construction of a mini domestic space (*Duplex I: The Petite-Bs Drawers*, 2023), while hungry caterpillars seem to have eaten through the installations that they inhabit (*Bedtime (after P. Thek)*, 2023; *The Dawn of Everything*, 2023). And as Touristes Tristes, both of them masticate chewing gum and then press it against various surfaces: an outdated metro map of Paris (*Untitled*, 2019), or a ceramic floor tile (*Step*, 2019). The act of chewing represents not only the artists' interest in the translation of materials from one to another but also the psychological rumination embodied in their works.

2 Océane Bruel's and dylan ray arnold's duo presentation 'Be Sure to Collect All Your Longings and Let Me Crash On Your Shore' at Glassbox, Paris, 17 May – 8 June 2019.

3 Press release for 'Be Sure to Collect All Your Longings and Let Me Crash On Your Shore'.

In their solo exhibition 'Growth of the Night Plants'[4], dylan ray arnold offered insight into how the hermetic figure's rumination serves as a 'generative, imaginative and necessary stopping off places for transformation'.[5] As for Océane Bruel, in 'hum'[6] she presented 'small material motifs – or syllables – of circular thoughts and feelings'. Chewing, in this sense, is drawn upon not only as a physical gesture, but also as the representation of thoughts that eat away at us, and how, in turn, we can stomach them.

What happens after the chewing? A long process of digestion, transformation and articulation. This brings us to the notion of time as material in the three practices at hand, and the importance of latency. Samuel Beckett wrote, 'The individual is the seat of a constant process of decantation, decantation from the vessel containing the fluid of future time, sluggish, pale and monochrome, to the vessel containing the fluid of past time, agitated and multicoloured by the phenomena of its hours.'[7] Océane's and dylan's works could thus illustrate the phenomena of hours, in all of its colours. The image of liquid being poured back and forth recalls the coming and going, the idea of a recycling or entangling of forms and ideas – not to mention the presence of coloured and murky liquids in several of their works, for instance Océane Bruel's *Sleeping Phrases (Overdrawn)* (2019) and *r-v-s-f-t* (2020) or Touristes Tristes' *untitled* (2020) or dylan ray arnold's *by the way* (2019). In their individual practices, each of the artists has developed a growing repertoire of works and fragments of works that are at times recycled, taking on second or even multiple lives in t practices that are deeply rooted in studio experimentation. This also holds true for their collaborative practice, as part of their methodology that defies the fixed meanings of things.

A birthday candle numbered 0 first appeared in Bruel's work *Dear Zero* (2019), before it found itself, half of what it used to be and hanging on by a thread, in a later installation for her solo exhibition 'L like Molecule' in 2020. Piggy banks, which first occurred in dylan ray arnold's installation *Fight Freeze (and a bit of relax rest digest)* (2020), have now appeared in a new configuration and installation in 'The Trouble and Trick of Being Together in the Season on Mists and Mellow Fruitfulness' alongside works by Bruel and the artist Iiris Kaarlehto (2023).

Roots of forms from works by Touristes Tristes at times also come to blossom in works by one of the artists individually. In their 2020 collaboration 'The Slow Business of Going', a sculpture-cum-support entitled *Pace of While* (2020) for the duo's publication *Paste of Time* time, again, seems to have been transformed into a series of floral sculptures featured in dylan's 'Growth of the Night Plants' (*Night Plant I*, 2023). Sinuous lines and curves also slither their way through each practice. In 'Be Sure To Collect All Your Longings...', layered and folded chewing gum is manipulated into what might evoke a pensive and crouching figure, like that of the thinker in art history. I am reminded of this figure in various forms presented by the artists, like in Océane's Là (2020), and dylan's *Ruminations on the contradictions of self-care, or drawer, folder, flower* (2023) or *And there is room in the bag of stars (solid company)* (2022). The introspective and affective body is suggested in silhouette. Through its absence it gives insight into how forms linger between the artists and undergo a long process of digestion, before arriving at a specific articulation that is ready to undergo the same cycle.

4 dylan ray arnold's solo exhibition, 'Growth of
the Night Plants' at Forum Box, Helsinki,
11 August – 3 September 2023.

5 Press release for 'Growth of the Night Plants'.

6 Océane Bruel's solo exhibition 'hum' at Pengerkatu 7 Työhuone, Helsinki, 5–21 May 2022.

5 Press release for 'Growth of the Night Plants'.

6 Océane Bruel's solo exhibition 'hum' at Pengerkatu 7 Työhuone, Helsinki, 5–21 May 2022.

7 Samuel Beckett, cited in Hunter Dukes, 'Beck-
ett's Vessels and the Animation of Containers',
Journal of Modern Literature, Vol. 40, No. 4
(Summer 2017), pp. 75–89.

The articulation of all three practices often happens through the assemblage of objects – both found and manipulated – and ideas. The gestures are precise, transformative and deeply intuitive. Océane Bruel's installations often unfold across a space riddled with works serving as punctuation in a visual language that expresses her sensibility to the everyday and the emotions entangled within it. This is seen, for instance, in her series of ceramic scribbles that stand as a confusing full stop to a sentence of four oil pastel drawings (*hum*, 2022). dylan ray arnold, on the other hand, articulates the psychology that shapes the everyday rather than the emotions that inhabit it. In complex drawings, collages and sculptures – microcosms of psychedelic domestic spaces composed of elements of the quotidian – dylan negotiates with their understanding of the nervous systems and its effects on mental processes. In *The Physical Dimensions of Consciousness with a Borrowed Blanket* (2023), a book of that title is tucked into a drawer as it pushes flowers from its slumber – bearing witness to a need for withdrawal for growth.

Cycles and systems crucial to the everyday, such as sleep cycles, weather cycles, nervous systems or immune systems, play a large part in the artists' individual and collaborative efforts of articulation. If we understand articulation in its definition as the state of being jointed, we can understand how their works address the corporeality of the everyday. Their investigations into our relationship with objects and spaces reveal how bodies are vessels of affect – of all the unnoticed minuscule and molecular events – and how they operate in the world.

[...] affect is persistent proof of a body's never less than ongoing immersion in and among the world's obstinacies and rhythms, its refusals as much as its invitations. Affect can be understood then as a gradient of bodily capacity [...] that rises and falls not only along various rhythms and modalities of encounter but also through the troughs and sieves of sensation and sensibility, an incrementalism that coincides with belonging to comportments of matter of virtually any and every sort.[8]

8 Gregory J. Seigworth and Melissa Gregg, 'An Inventory of Shimmers', in *The Affect Theory Reader*, Durham & London, Duke University Press, 2010, pp. 1–2.

9 Press release for dylan ray arnold's solo exhibition 'Nervous System(s), snooze(in9)' at Kunsthalle Turku, 21 February – 22 March 2020.

Folding affect into matter is yet another gesture that Océane and dylan share and explore together, sometimes quite literally. For our first collaboration in 2019, Océane folded sentimental objects of mine into a package whose envelope was made from an uncooked ceramic mould of bubble wrap. The delicately packed secret eventually faced its demise when pests attacked the organic matter it once concealed. In dylan's work, folds appear not only through gesture but also as a motif. For their exhibition 'Nervous System(s), snooze(in9)' they wrote, 'the works are wrinkles in a strained world where resources, explanations, and meaning are at once plentiful and scarce.'[9] Folds, or wrinkles, are explored in their capacity to resist and conceal, envelope and protect.

Side by side, three works perfectly illustrate the receptive multilingualism of Océane Bruel and dylan ray arnold, not only in their form but in their use of chewing, articulating and folding. These are Océane Bruel's *al solito posto sera* (2020), dylan ray arnold's *Metabolic Silhouette* (2023) and Touristes Tristes' *Body Doubles* (2018–21). All are floor installations – a standard practice for the artists – with a delineated space in pale yellow – a familiar colour for them. The works evoke the presence of a ruminating body.

Océane's piece – thin waxed yellow fabric full of creases upon which sit a knife and a ceramic lemon – reminds me of what I once described as 'sticky sheets, and the mixing of sweat. Feverish, summery, sick sweat'[10] or the place of a body fighting sleep or an eventful reverie. Yet the body is absent. In *Metabolic Silhouette*, dylan laid an anthropomorphic figure articulated by wooden flowers and a complex ceramic digestive system to rest on a yellow towel, summoning metabolic and mental processes. *Body Doubles* can therefore be understood as the perfect derivation of the other practices. Composed of two moulds of garment bags (folding) made with recycled silicone from previous productions, the body is suggested not only in the title, but also in the pistachio shells (chewing) that become eyes, and in the candy mouth smoking a cigarette that could easily go unnoticed by the non-attentive viewer. Océane's preferred suggested body combines with dylan's often present – albeit fragmented – body as they merge their ways of working. This reveals how, perhaps, their collaboration allows for a certain freedom that the other has yet to explore alone.

Together and apart, Océane Bruel and dylan ray arnold present us with a material poetic approach to understanding the everyday and all that it entails. Their languages use objects and materials in a partition of gestures to translate the human experience: an experience that cycles through joy, grief, pleasure, sadness, anxiety, calmness, and so on. Often inhabited by familiar objects – affective and sticky objects to cite Sarah Ahmed – their works evoke elusive and strangely relatable sensations. This phantom experience is summed up perfectly in a poem by Jimmie Durham.

10 After visiting Océane Bruel's exhibition 'L like Molecule' I wrote a short response to it. Available at: https://www.katiaporro.com/dear-zero/

11 Jimmie Durham, 'Object' [1964], published in Laura Mulvey, *Fetishism and Curiosity* (Bloomington and Indianapolis: Indiana University Press, 1996), p. 175.

It must have been an odd object to begin with.
Now the ghosts of its uses
Whisper around my head, tickle the tips
Of my fingers. Weeds
Reclaim with quick silence the beams, pillars
Doorways. Places change, and a small object
Stands defiant in its placelessness.
Durable because it contains intensely meanings
Which it can no longer pour out.[11]

       Similar to how the bearer of fables and companion lovers reactivate words after a loss of meaning in Wittig's fictional world, Océane Bruel and dylan ray arnold revive the object's whisper and its tickle on the tips of the fingers when it can no longer pour out meaning on its own.

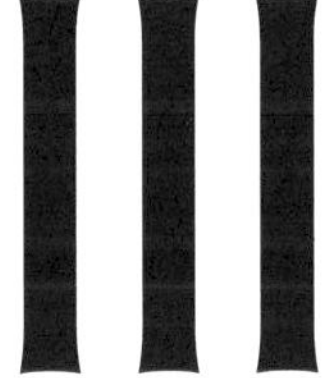

First Things First

Anders Kreuger

Anders Kreuger is a Swedish-born curator, writer, editor and educator based in Helsinki, with over 25 years of international experience in the contemporary art field. He is Director of Kohta, an artist-initiated private kunsthalle for Helsinki inaugurated in 2017. In 2010–19 he was Senior Curator at M HKA, the Museum of Contemporary Art Antwerp, and in 2012–18 a member of the editorial team for the London-based art journal *Afterall*. In 2007–10 Kreuger was Director of the Malmö Art Academy, Lund University, Sweden, and at the same time Exhibitions Curator at Lunds konsthall. In 1997–99 he was Founding Director of NIFCA, the Nordic Institute for Contemporary Art, in Helsinki. Recent exhibitions outside Kohta include 'Aslan Goisum: Prism' (Lunds konsthall, 2024) and 'The Meeting That Never Was' (MO Museum, Vilnius, 2022–23, co-curated with Charles Esche and Gabrielė Radzevičiūtė).

One question that we ask of artists is this: How can we make sense of life through form? We expect them to exercise as much freedom as they can grab to help us answer it. They should use all available tricks of observation and association, deduction and induction, contradiction and dissimulation. They should piece together the meticulously designed with the randomly encountered in ever new combinations from which meaning – the meaning of life! – might be extracted.

A reliable method for creating form is to construct dichotomies, oppositional pairs that help us organise a flow of intuitions into visibly clashing positions. Dichotomies are so explicit and self-contained that we often feel an urge to break them apart and rearrange their now-intelligible meaning as a field of multiple possibilities. Part of what we expect artists to do for us is to guide us through such processes of composition and decomposition. And they do it all the time, weaving and unravelling oppositions between flows of emotion and fields of interest, intuited and explicated meaning, closed and open form.

This is another way of saying that artists matter to all of us in society, far beyond the province of the arts where they mostly dwell. It is also a way of introducing a dichotomy that, I feel, conditions this entire book. Almost a quarter-century into the new Millennium it is difficult, perhaps futile, to discuss artist residencies or mobility programmes for artists (or indeed any other aspect of international activity within the arts) without spelling out the opposition between two of their political premises. On the one hand, promoting artistic freedom, specifically artists' freedom to travel. On the other hand, containing the climate crisis by restricting non-essential travel and other forms of over-consumption.

Although the topic of artist residencies may seem technical or peripheral to many who are not directly involved in it, it directly illustrates a fundamental clash of ambitions that is far from trivial. How shall the needs of human society be weighed against the needs of the planet that sustains it? Freedom, also in its artistic form, is existential to humans, but so is the survival of the planet. For now its fate seems to depend on us. How shall we, in this situation, exercise our freedom? What consequences shall we expect from what we choose to do or not to do?

I will offer subjective reflection on four aspects of this conundrum. Remembering the 1970s metaphor of 'digging where you stand', I will try to stay as close as possible to the question this book is asking: How are the narratives of artist residencies changing? Yet I will also try to stay outside of the 'politics of mentioning' by avoiding the evaluation of concrete institutions or initiatives. I wish to discuss, not to blame or praise.

OBLIGATION/FREEDOM

It is out of this I want to propose an existential creativity. How do I define it? It is the creativity wherein nothing should be wasted. As a writer, it means everything I write should be directed to the immediate end of drawing attention to the dire position we are in as a species. It means that the writing must have no frills. I should speak only truth. In it, the truth must be also beauty. It calls for the highest economy. It means everything I do must have a singular purpose.[1]

1 Ben Okri, 'Artists must confront the climate crisis – we must write as if these are the last days', *The Guardian*, 12 November 2021, https://www.theguardian.com/commentisfree/2021/nov/12/artists-climate-crisis-write-creativity-imagination (accessed in February 2024).

The 'existential creativity' – or could it be 'creative existentialism'? – proposed by the celebrated Nigerian-English writer Ben Okri makes sense, the same kind of sense as any artistic programme based on justified moral outrage and informed political opinion makes. He doesn't issue any prohibition against aesthetic practice, which for him equals writing. He doesn't retool Theodor W Adorno's post-war dictum – 'to write poetry after Auschwitz is barbaric' – for the climate cataclysm, but he does call for the instrumentalisation of all artistic creativity, as an act of free will prompted by the obligation to act responsibly in threatening circumstances. An obligation that should be apparent to all. 'We need a new art to waken people both to the enormity of what is looming and the fact that we can still do something about it.'[2]

The sense that this makes is one that appeals to our political mind, if such a thing exists (and I hope it does). Surely it is

2 Ibid.

reasonable to ask everyone self-identifying as a creative agent for a voluntary contribution towards the common goal of slowing the Sixth Extinction that is already underway. Surely the world could still become a better place if we all suspended those parts of our free will that push us into vainglory, if we got together and pooled our mental and material resources to form a truly educational 'new art' that would 'speak only truth' and therefore would be not just understandable but also acceptable, indeed desirable, to all.

Isn't this how art was always supposed to be? At least it is what many have wished for, from the depths of antiquity to Bertolt Brecht and (in their specific way, by way of 'make friends not art') the Indonesian artist collective ruangrupa that curated Documenta 15: an arena for common action, societal catharsis and public instruction where the 'severe style' and 'anything goes' are fellow travellers because the ends always justify the means.

This can be achieved, and it has been, as Imperial Art of a myriad kinds, from ancient Egypt to the Soviet Union and its satellites, as visual theology and as mass-produced entertainment. The aesthetic and ethical hazards that accompany any such insistence on the usefulness of art, whether imposed from above by sacred or secular authorities or rising from among the ranks of art practitioners and audiences, are well known but nonetheless easy for each new generation to forget.

Isn't the situation now so dire that zero-waste singularity of purpose is called for, as Okri is doing, and that resistance against it amounts to little more than a flare-up of obsolete bourgeois individualism, an unwillingness to sacrifice one's comfort or privileges for the common good?

You will already have guessed that I can't quite subscribe to this opinion. The freedom of artists to challenge or simply ignore the political mind, their own and others, remains a counterweight to the abuse of the truth-as-beauty rulebook that will always happen and should come as no surprise. The powers of creation and judgment, intuition and invention that the best artists possess will always find ways to bypass any rules that someone else tries to impose on them. This is among the most valuable gifts that the individual can offer the collective, and certainly one of the recurrent selling points of art.

CREATION/JUDGMENT

When I was making 'Intuitive Exhibition' I wanted to go beyond the heritage of Duchamp, who taught us once and for all that any object, like the saw I was talking about, may be considered from at least two points of view: by its function or as a ready-made work of art. For me, this is a totally Western view of things. In another continent this saw could already be a symbol of power. It could be a taboo object. If we go into space, we could encounter animals who are exactly like this saw. A red bird, for example. There's that reference. I called it 'Intuitive Exhibition' in the sense that until now, through our great predecessors like Duchamp, invention has replaced composition. Many modern artists are more attached to invention. But I propose – and practice – that intuition should replace invention.[3]

3 Anders Kreuger and Irmeline Lebeer (eds), *Robert Filliou: The Secret of Permanent Creation*. (Antwerp: M HKA, Brussels: Editions Lebeer-Hossmann and Milan: Mousse Publishing, 2017), p. 101.

The French-American artist, poet and playwright Robert Filliou (1926–87) was the hitherto unsurpassed theorist of artistic research, an attitude and activity that he adopted already around 1970.

Research is not the exclusive privilege of those who know. Rather, it is the domain of those who don't know. Each time we turn to something that we don't understand – cats, for example, water, anger, hair, injustice, trees – we are doing research.[4]

4 Ibid. p.152.

Filliou's practice – or, as he would have put it, his 'making and doing' – yielded a string of new coinages such as 'permanent creation', 'teaching and learning as performance arts', 'mind-openers' or 'the speed of art'. Yet despite his deep aversion against negative pronouncements, his legacy is perhaps even more significant for all the things he disavowed by pointing out

5 See for instance the American collector Walter Conrad Arensberg's role in launching Duchamp's *Fountain* in 2017, as referred to in passing by Thierry de Duve in his essay 'This Is Art: Anatomy of a Sentence', *Artforum International*, April 2014.

better alternatives. A close reading of the quote above reveals that Filliou is effectively demolishing the cult of Duchamp as the inscrutable arbiter and disruptor of the West's own art system. This myth, in turn, conveniently skates over the role Duchamp always reserved for the art market in his provocations.[5] Filliou calls him out as a pillar of this Western hegemony over art and artists, and at the same time swings an implicit sledgehammer at one of its fundaments: the priority of judgment over creation for deciding what constitutes a work of art. (And, we should add, for what a work of art is supposed and allowed to do.)

6 Robert Filliou, *Teaching and Learning as Performance Arts.* Cologne and New York: Verlag Gebr. König, 1970 (Facsimile republished by Occasional Papers, London, 2014), p. 191. Marianne (Staffeldt) is Filliou's Danish-born wife. *Dépaysement* means 'change of scenery'.

I venture to explicate this critique, which Filliou kept partially under wraps, because I think his notion of 'invention' may be read as 'the constant invention of new ways of judging that anything is or can be art' and 'intuition' as another way of saying 'permanent creation'. In his notes for the travelling *Poïpoïdrome* project, which aimed at integrating African philosophy and Western performance art, Filliou writes:

As Marianne – tired by the artistic quarrels and double-dealings she so frequently witnesses – told me once: 'You're artists only when you create. Once you're thru creating you're not artists anymore.' That's right. Creation is not enough. One must not stop creating. One can't afford to. That's right, I thought. What I must share with everyone is the knack of permanent creation. An Institute of Permanent Creation. Based on fun, and humour, and *dépaysement*, and good will and participation.[6]

7 See Immanuel Kant, *Critique of the Power of Judgment* (transl. and eds Paul Guyer and Allen W Wood) (Cambridge University Press, 1998).

Western society has, at least since the Enlightenment, privileged the critical reception of culture-as-product over the democratic co-creation of culture-as-process. Immanuel Kant, the philosopher who made it his task to define the nature of enlightenment, famously insisted on the explanatory priority of judgments over concepts. Indeed, since his *Critique of the Power of Judgment* appeared in 1790[7], Western thought has been focused on the methodological and moral necessity of the act of judgment for society as a whole, and for the arts in particular.

Everyone was to be equal in front of the law, and no one was to shirk responsibility by asking 'Who am I to judge?'

One often-overlooked positive side effect is that prioritising the act of judgment renders the preparations for that act, especially the elaboration of quantitative and qualitative criteria for judgment, less crucial than contemporary bureaucracy would have us believe. Incidentally, this is something cultural organisations would do well to remember whenever they are asked to formulate measurable criteria for their decision-making. Yet although resistance to quantitative methods of evaluation may help us problematise judgment as part of our Kantian cultural heritage, the crucial issue is more fundamental.

Kant's rather pedantic categorisation of 'sensory', 'ethical' and 'subjective universal' judgment of 'the agreeable', 'the good', 'the beautiful' and 'the sublime' has deflected attention from the actual condition for all aesthetic judgment, namely that humans lack reliable channels for sharing sensory data with each other. If we will never know what anyone else sees, hears and tastes, how can we judge such matters with any authority?

The dominant role that judgment, and more specifically critical judgment, plays in a Western art system – which, among many other things, has produced artist residencies – frequently leads to a conflation of ethical judgment with its aesthetic counterpart. This is problematic not only because aesthetic judgment itself is further problematised by such unclarity, but more specifically because of the built-in ambiguity of widespread forms of contemporary creation such as artistic research or socially engaged art.

The resulting confusion has made critical debate about such art forms all but impossible. Should we judge them for their possible societal relevance, methodological efficiency and moral usefulness – which, by the way, is usually much less easy than it might seem – or should we endeavour to somehow isolate their 'intra-aesthetic identity' from their 'extra-aesthetic content'? I believe that these practices should be considered as creation first and foremost. They are, after all, aiming at being included in the Western art system, and we therefore have not only the right, but also the obligation to judge them as part of it.

This excursion will, I hope, have prepared us for a return to the ideological core of our topic, as it is increasingly formulated in Finland and other Northern European democracies. Should climate crisis, the objective condition of the world, form the theoretical and operational horizon for artist residencies and other ways of promoting and supporting artists? Or should the basis for all work with, for and through artists instead be artistic freedom, a necessarily subjective notion? Should the political mind take precedence over the power of creation, or is any query into a hierarchic relationship between them just a misuse of mental energy? Perhaps it is an example of a dichotomy that may be a useful tool for illustrating and illuminating a problem but not for dissecting its anatomy.

ANSWERABILITY/WITHDRAWAL

A large portion of the carbon footprint consisted of the flights of the artists and the Biennial organisation. [...] The total carbon footprint of the event corresponds to the annual emissions of 100 Finns. If the carbon footprint is set in proportion to the number of visitors, the emissions per visitor are 7 kg, which is approximately 0.07% of the average annual carbon footprint of a Finn. It should be noted that the average carbon footprint of Finns is among the largest in Europe.[8]

8 Heidi Taskinen (ed.), *Impact Study of the Helsinki Biennial 2021* (Helsinki: City of Helsinki, Executive Office, Urban Research and Statistics, 2022), p. 30.

It has, in recent years, become a commonplace that the arts have a share in the overriding human responsibility for healing the planet, and the role usually assigned to them is to raise awareness, in innovative ways attractive to the wider population. Nevertheless, this is only one of the reasons why money and other resources continue to be spent on art and artists. Cultural policy is always hybrid; it is an applied art, as it were (and not only because it hinges on applying for grants). This doesn't imply that its 'green' rhetoric is insincere, only that it is, precisely, rhetorical – and that the sincerity of those who use it to define their identity as practitioners may be as problematic as the policy goals of those who use it to condition their attention and funding.

I'm proposing the metaphor of answerability in response to the demands posed by judgment. The practitioners who make up the art system of a contemporary society (of the developed variety that Finland proudly exemplifies) have learned to internalise its various demands to prove the usefulness of what they are making and doing. They tend to express themselves by appealing to a higher purpose, such as healing the planet. By contrast, the metaphor of withdrawal hints at other reasons for becoming and being an artist, and for supporting artists. It is as if those other reasons – among them the individual and collective desire for visibility in the world at large – had been retired from immediate view and should no longer be talked about openly, at least in some influential segments of the same art system.

That is why I, a not-so-innocent bystander, barely lifted my eyebrows when I learned that the Helsinki Biennial 2021 was declared an overwhelming success.[9] No one would expect the official Impact Study to acknowledge that the biennial was so on-message about the climate crisis that its institutional identity as a contemporary art event was at risk of being diluted. Yet the study also plays down its observable environmental impact, both globally through emissions and locally through wear and tear to the delicate ecosystem on the island of Vallisaari. That is more predictable that it should be, and not just because of political and economic concerns. The first biennial, to be followed by a second edition in the summer of 2023, is emblematic of the ideological dilemma I have just tried to capture. The two good reasons for its existence are, alas, not easily reconciled: promoting awareness through art and promoting awareness of art.

My overall judgment is that the first Helsinki Biennial came dangerously close to confusing ethical ambition with aesthetic achievement, and thus to damaging its visibility on the international arena that all biennials of this size and cost are playing for. This statement is easy to dismiss as a reflection of elitist internationalism, but I offer it to underline my point that the unspoken priorities of art events (and initiatives, and institutions) matter more than many want to acknowledge.

In countries like Finland and its neighbours – sparsely populated and dependent on exports but remote from markets –

9 Ibid., p.4.

it is hard to escape that the arts, and the policies that promote them, will be answering to economic and geopolitical realities first and foremost. There will always be strong yearnings to be noticed and acknowledged by a quantifiable amount of others from an unspecified elsewhere, to forestall still-dreaded cultural isolation and almost to prove to yourself that you exist in the world. So when arts organisations in the Nordic region insist on slow travelling, wishing to set good examples of responsible governance and resource management, they risk limiting their impact to areas that are reachable without flying, but at the same time too similar in outlook to really make a difference as international partners. On the other hand, they risk coming across as hypocritical when they make exceptions from such ethically motivated self-imposed rules, which they will all have to do from time to time. Keeping more than one thought in your head is one of the best strategies against dichotomies.

CAREFREENESS/RESPONSIBILITY

Woken, I lay in the arms of my own warmth and listened
To a storm enjoying its storminess in the winter dark
Till my ear, as it can when half-asleep or half-sober,
Set to work to unscramble that interjectory uproar,
Construing its airy vowels and watery consonants
Into a love-speech indicative of a Proper Name.

Scarcely the tongue I should have chosen, yet, as well
As harshness and clumsiness would allow, it spoke in your praise,
Kenning you a god-child of the Moon and the West Wind
With a power to tame both real and imaginary monsters,
Likening your poise of being to an upland county,
Here green on purpose, there pure blue for luck.

Loud though it was, alone as it certainly found me,
It reconstructed a day of peculiar silence
When a sneeze could be heard a mile off, and had me walking
On a headland of lava beside you, the occasion as ageless
As the stare of any rose, your presence exactly
So once, so valuable, so very now.

This, moreover, at an hour when only too often
A smirking devil annoys me in beautiful English,
Predicting a world where every sacred location
Is a sand-buried site all cultured Texans do,
Misinformed and thoroughly fleeced by their guides,
And gentle hearts are extinct like Hegelian Bishops.

Grateful, I slept till a morning that would not say
How much it believed of what I said the storm had said
But quietly drew my attention to what had been done
– So many cubic metres the more in my cistern
Against a leonine summer –, putting first things first:
Thousands have lived without love, no one without water.[10]

10 W. H. Auden, 'First Things First', in Edward
   Mendelson (ed.), *W. H. Auden: Collected Poems*.
   (New York: Random House, 1976), pp. 444–45.

Written in 1956, when W H Auden was in his late forties and the Cold War the only thinkable reality, this beautiful and meaningful poem approaches apocalypse implicitly and, we may assume, in terms of thermo-nuclear annihilation rather than other kinds of man-made environmental disasters ('a world where every sacred location is a sand-buried site all cultured Texans do'). Nevertheless, 'First Things First' offers readers a string of visions of loss, experienced as well as anticipated, and crystalline images of nature ('an upland county, here green on purpose, there pure blue for luck') that rhyme only too well with today's climate anxiety. Moreover, in the iconic last line Auden demonstrates how to break up dichotomies into mind-opening flows. He reveals his own opposition of love, the supreme manifestation of human freedom, to water, without which everything else becomes unthinkable, to be an absurd dilemma, impossible to overcome meaningfully but somehow possible to formulate beautifully.

With all this I want to say something that is rather simple, but perhaps not so easy to accept. Everyone who works 'with for and through' artists should begin by trusting them to do the right thing. Accomplished artists are highly aware of what is going on with the world and what they are able to do about it. Within the frames they set for their work they have learned to observe, understand, animate and subvert. I would go even further. Exhibition curators, museum directors or residency managers should assume that artists know what is best for the world, and that they know better than anyone else how to articulate this knowledge and how to act on it. That is how the art system can help strengthen the position of art in society at large, and thereby society itself.

If this sounds like a naïvely carefree approach that will make it difficult to achieve the carbon-neutral biennial or the public programme that produces knowledge about hospitality or contamination or inter-species solidarity or other topics designed to raise awareness of how to heal the planet, then maybe it is because it starts from another idea of what the art system should do with its excess energy and unrealised ambition. Just like Auden's 'airy vowels and watery consonants' paint a more convincing picture than any thousand words on climate change and artistic freedom, so the art institution that puts artists at the core of all its programming and builds all its structures around them will, in my version of things, be able to shoulder more responsibility for revealing what the arts can achieve with all its agendas, explicated or not.

It is not that art and artists need to be protected from demands for responsible action and sheltered and pampered inside the province of the arts, of artistic freedom as it were. Quite the opposite, what I am arguing is that society should tear down its boundaries towards art. In a time of great danger, when fears of a thermo-nuclear holocaust are again being stoked, we should finally open ourselves to the forms that artists propose to help us see meaning and, yes, beauty in the world.

Education = Residation? Art Schools as Residencies and Safe Spaces for Artists

Vytautas Michelkevičius

Dr. Vytautas Michelkevičius is a curator, writer, educator and researcher based in Vilnius. He holds a PhD from the Vilnius Academy of Arts, where he is Professor and Head of the Photography, Animation and Media Art Department and of the Doctoral Programme in the Arts. In 2010–19 he served as artistic director of the Nida Art Colony in Lithuania. Dr. Michelkevičius's focus is on media art and theory, as well as the social conditions of artists, artist residencies and artistic research. Recent curatorial projects include 'When the wind blows from the East, we make art and (sur)render reality' (Ars Electronica, Linz, 2022) and Dainius Liškevičius's exhibition 'Museum' (Lithuanian Pavilion, Venice Biennale, 2015). Recent publications include *Impact of Artistic Research on Humanities and Contemporary Art* (with Aldis Gedutis, 2023–24), *Atlas of Diagrammatic Imagination: Maps in Research, Art and Education* (co-edited with Lina Michelkevičė, 2019) and *Mapping Artistic Research: Towards Diagrammatic Knowledge* (2018).

ONE, TWO, THREE AND I'M FREE!

Every time I look back from my residency studio to my careless days in art school I realise: that was my best residency ever. I had access to workshops and studios 24/7 or at least twelve hours a day. I had plenty of time. I made one artwork per semester or even academic year (yes, really!). I had instant feedback and discursivity, visiting professors and curators were giving abundant advice and I was swimming in the appreciation and I was getting a lot of soft sawder – nice but probably not very sincere compliments.

But I was still discontented and constantly dreaming about freedom after graduation, working without supervision and hopping from one residency to another, from Canada to Brazil and from Chile to Taiwan.

These good days are over. Despite having my honours diploma issued in fancy handwriting, I'm sitting in a remote residency in a village somewhere in Germany or Italy, formerly a famous artist colony, and the cold breeze ruffles my sketches every time a visiting curator opens my studio door. I have insomnia or a headache after a get-together party with newly arrived residents. And my gallerist is constantly sending to me messenger/whatsapp/telegram messages with silly GIFs and emoticons, trying to stimulate my creativity. The residency is self-financed and I have to send a new work every week to my greedy gallerist to pay my bills. However, I am happy to be away from my partner, pet and artist friends for a while…

At this point, if I'm a recent graduate, should I take a (another) loan, get my MA and jump onto the doctoral pedestal?

– Semi-fake testimony by a young, but too slowly emerging artist

1 The 'Global East' concept was coined by Martin Müller in 2020. These are the countries that used to be the Second World (the Socialist and Soviet bloc) and are now fluctuating between the past and the future. They have very different recent his(stories) of trying to develop and catch up with the Global North, while some of them are tilting towards the Global South and all the problems signalled by this notion, including fragile democracies, difficult socio-economic situations, post-colonial issues, and very little investment in art, culture and education, etc. 'The East is too rich to be a proper part of the South, but too poor to be a part of the North. It is too powerful to be periphery, but too weak to be the centre.' Martin Müller, 'In Search of the Global East: Thinking between North and South', *Geopolitics*, 25:3 (2020), p. 734.

This essay uncovers two quite vivid trends in the residency world: finding links with the academy and carrying out artistic research while in residency. Most of my thoughts are based on 15 years of practice working as a curator, educator and researcher in a specific region: the Global East[1] and, if we narrow it down, North-Eastern Europe. But these insights might be also applicable elsewhere.

The relationship between the residency and the academy has not been investigated too much but it is easy to find parallels between these two, both as hosting bodies (sites) and as centres of activity where artists' careers, skills and mindsets are developed. Both of them are based on strong communal sentiments. While residencies bring artists together for a shorter time (1–12 months), academies form longer-lasting, although still temporary, communities of younger and elder artists and critical thinkers.

Moreover, we may notice the recent trend that art academies in Central-Eastern and Northern Europe become shelters for a large number of Ukrainian refugee artists, just as they hosted increasing numbers of young artists from Belarus or Afghanistan during the last decade.

In this essay I want to investigate the relationship between these two modes of hosting artists and facilitating their creative and thinking powers, the academy and the residency. One more question remains lingering: How does artistic research empower and liberate artists today and what is its relation to mobility and residencies?

WHAT IS THE ROLE OF ART SCHOOLS IN THE CONTEXT OF MOBILITY AND RESIDENCES?

In recent decades European art schools, art academies and art universities are becoming shelters for more and more artists, coming from the Global South and the Global East. This is noticeable to anyone travelling to these educational establishments and meeting these artists in conferences, workshops and exhibitions. What if we consider these establishments long-term residency programmes?

Unlike elitist old-school academies, their contemporary counterparts accept people from various backgrounds. It no longer matters if you have graduated as an engineer, a philosopher, a social scientist or a lawyer. This might be called inter-disciplinary mobility. People coming from a variety of backgrounds enrich artistic practice as a field of knowledge with very different competences from various fields. Since contemporary artistic practice is very open to receiving influences from other disciplines, it also serves as an accumulative field of knowledge and a platform where these disciplines meet.

We know that every artist is an explorer, but not every artist is a researcher. Those artists who involve themselves in epistemic discussions, test the limits of disciplines, accumulate knowledge and produce new insights based on that may end up as with a doctor of arts (DA) or doctor of philosophy (PhD) diploma. Yet it is also totally fine if you just graduate with a BA or an MA. It depends on your goals and needs. The MFA (Master of Fine Arts) is no longer a terminal degree for artists, although some schools (in the USA and some other countries) still try to claim that.

What happens if we consider BA, MA and PhD programmes to be three different kinds of residencies? Anything goes while you are pursuing your BA degree. Curiosity is boiling over the pot and you try to attend as many different classes and workshops as possible. All those BA years are a never-ending party. You attend exhibitions, performances, festivals mostly as a participant and always complain that you don't have enough time.

You slow down when you enter the MA programme and try to be more focused and orient everything to your projects or interests. You also meet peers of various ages and more diverse backgrounds, which enriches the learning environment. In recent years MA or MFA programmes have tended to become a more like residencies for experienced artists returning to the academy five, ten or even twenty years after finishing their BAs. Or sometimes MA students enter art school for the first time in their lives after having studied science, engineering, philosophy, languages or anything else but art for their BAs. They may have been practising art without calling it art, and they may have collected quite solid artistic portfolios that enable them to enter MA programmes.

At least in most of the Nordic and Baltic art academies you meet MA students who are in their 30s or 40s, searching for a discursive community and a relevant research environment that will give them feedback. Care is needed for late emerging and early mid-career artists. After all the institutional critique, academies are again becoming safe spaces for artists and their experimentations off the beaten (gallery) track. Where else if not in the academy studio can you experiment secretly (from your peers) and freely (away from the market) and dive into new fields of artistic endeavours or research?

If you wonder why an MA programme should be considered a long-term residency programme, you have the right to be doubtful. Let's forget the old-school academic model where you attend the master classes of a genius professor and meet every week or month in ritual-like circles and praise each other's artworks and their deepness and rhizomic relationality with art history and philosophy and very seldom society at large. Some MA programmes may be considered residency programmes because they are socially oriented and led by artists, curators or educators who believe in the artist's power to change, influence or criticise their immediate environment and society at large. They are functioning from Helsinki to Oslo and from Vilnius to Vienna. In most cases such education is free but at the same time highly competitive.

Some of these programmes focus on public space, some on the environment, the climate or other urgent issues, some of them are very broadly called MAs in 'fine art', 'media art' or 'arts and crafts'. Unlike in residency programmes, housing is not the main focus in MA programmes. In most cases academies provide at least shared studio space. But certainly, an MA programme may become a centre of attraction or a main reason to reside in a city or country. An MA programme may provide the safe space and the context to act as an artist and develop your skills, career and networks.

There are various ways for such programmes to organise their curricula. Methods that make them similar to residencies are artist talks, lectures and workshops, curator visits, open studios, interventions in public space, various professional trips and visits and fieldwork. But what happens when artists graduate from an MA programme and still want to stay close to the academy?

DOCTORAL PROGRAMMES AS LONG-TERM RESIDENCY OPPORTUNITIES

In the 2020s, the third decade of the twenty-first century, everybody is aware that art academies and art universities will not be able to avoid the flood wave of artistic research that is mostly instrumentalised within third-cycle programmes. Quite a few artists (and designers, architects, curators, writers and others) carry out practice-based research projects and defend them as dissertations. If we observe these programmes from a residency perspective, some of them come across as very long and professionalised residency programmes providing participants with studios, grants (although not always), access to various workshops, involvement in large professional and research networks; and, finally, with supervisors and peers who make up a professional community. The only thing missing is accommodation, but if the doctoral grant is substantial it would also allow participants to rent a flat. By comparison, there are a few dozen residency programmes in the world that last from six to twelve months, but so far probably none of them would host artists for three to five years.

If you go through various programmes in the EU (whether in Vienna, Helsinki or Vilnius) you will meet many artists who moved to that city only because of the doctoral programme. The artists are from all over the world, including the Global South and the Global East, which means that artistic research is giving opportunities to artists who have fewer professional opportunities in their home countries.

Therefore, art academies and art universities take on a new but very important role in the art market.[2] Moreover, the research market (as an ecosystem of its own with its funding and dissemination structures like journals and conferences) is also slowly becoming populated and enriched by a new kind of researcher: artists who (re)invent methodologies of both the humanities and the social sciences and sometimes even the natural sciences.

What do doctoral programmes provide that is outside the scope of usual residency programmes? First, they offer long-term stability and certainty about your future as an artist, at least for a few years while you are in the programme. They also foster your epistemic curiosity and

2 The 'market' is here understood as any context where artist are employed and being paid for their professional work based on their artistic practice and skills, be it a gallery, school, social centre, business entity or research institute.

give access to resources related to both knowledge and skills. Most academies and universities have access to libraries and vast electronic databases, and moreover to workshops with skilled technicians. Of course, some residencies also offer workshops, but they usually can't offer the same diversity of disciplines, equipment or materials.

So, are doctoral programmes ideal and better than residency programmes? Of course not. I already hear complaints that these doctoral programmes bring nothing but the academisation of artistic practice. But what is 'academisation' really? I think we should differentiate between historical academies, which are safe havens for storing and keeping traditions and skills, and contemporary academies, which are open for critical discussions, discursivity and questioning what art, society and culture is.

Fewer and fewer art school teachers urge their students to follow a certain art cannon – which is what I mean by 'academisation'. I agree that there are plenty of old-school and conservative academies that limit creativity, focus on skills rather than ideas and constrain discursive discussions or even downgrade theory and philosophy. Luckily, most of these academies don't have third-cycle education programmes, because they simply don't believe in them. Moreover, they are probably afraid of any kind of innovation. Let them stay safely in their traditional models of education and masterclasses.

When we put contemporary art schools (mostly art universities) in focus, we see that the advantage of their doctoral programmes is that they empower artists in society, acknowledge their working and research methods in the context of other (more traditional) modes of knowledge production and provide future careers for artists in education and research sectors next to the already existing art scene. This is how academies take up the role as a social hubs advancing artists' careers, while at the same time offering some services that used to be provided mainly by art residency programmes.

Of course, these doctoral programmes are not for every artist, and they are as competitive as most of the funded residencies. Even those with no adjacent funding, among them the programmes in Linz (Austria), Weimar (Germany) or Helsinki are quite competitive.

These doctoral programmes also change the artistic life in each specific city and make it more vibrant and international. Artists from all over the world come to these programmes and stay in town for a while. Their diverse worldviews and epistemic beliefs spread in the hosting cities and campuses. These environments become sites of investigation and research and their outcomes spill over into global networks.

GEOPOLITICAL MOMENTS AND DETOURS: RESIDENCY AS A SAFE SPACE OR REFUGE FROM EVERYDAY DISASTERS AND PERTURBATIONS

Residency may be defined not only in the physical sense but also in the mental sense of a place where you feel safe or welcomed with all your worldviews, minority-related issues or doubts. We know that some countries are democratic, some autocratic and some in-between. Residencies can be those hospitable countries which at least temporarily host artists at risk.

However, this concept has become quite sensitive nowadays. In the light of almost ten years of war in Ukraine, many cultural managers are unsure if they can accept artists from the aggressor country (Russia and partly Belarus), when at the same time many artists from partly occupied Ukraine need their help more. These ethical questions also come up during other conflicts all around the world.

For decades, residencies have been safe spaces for artists with different worldviews and beliefs escaping the harsh, unfriendly or unfree environment they live in. Remote residencies have been shelters and survival points allowing artists to recover after deprivation or harsh living conditions. At the same time they were hideaways from roaring urban life and unbearable everyday routines. Recently they have also become retreats from financial and career-driven pressure and from project- or goal-oriented lifestyles. One can argue that all these problems are first-world problems, and that we should first welcome artists at great(er) risk, escaping war and harsh regimes. How to redefine the role of residencies so that they may accommodate such fragilities, is one of the biggest challenges of the recent decade.

To sum up, in recent decades the Global North has accommodated more and more artists from the Global South and the Global East who first moved to the new host countries because of residency programmes or studies (at BA, MA or PhD level) and later got into their local art scenes and relocated for a longer period of time. Therefore, art academies and universities can also be treated as important players in the international mobility of artists and artworks.

In the beginning they act as temporary residencies or shelters in the safe country, assisting with visas and housing. Later some of the graduates may get employment as teachers, facilitators or workshop managers in the same schools or somewhere else. And after some more years you begin to feel their influence in local cultural life, not only through exhibitions and performances but also because of parties, music and food. I wish I could read a solid sociological account of how these incoming artists have changed their local scenes and made them richer, more diverse and globally connected, along the lines of what Richard Sennet wrote about NYC migrating artists communities in New York in the 1980s.

Additionally, there is a noticeable and influential flow from the West to the South and East when artists after graduating return to their home countries, change their local art scenes and contribute to their prosperity and development. The most known example could be ruangrupa, the curators of Documenta 15. Some of the group's members came back to Indonesia after studying abroad and contributed a lot to various scenes and projects there.

In recent decades, as the world has become more dangerous, art academies and art universities have joined residency programmes in becoming more and more active as hosts of artists in danger or at risk. Besides their principal function as providers of educational services, they have taken on residency functions more actively and visibly. Another significant trend is that art academies in northern, central and eastern Europe host more artists from neighbouring countries with authoritarian regimes or fragile democracies (Belarus, Ukraine, Russia, Armenia, Georgia, etc.) while the Nordic and Western European academies host artists from the Global South.

Bypassing Accumulation: Residencies as Mobile Assemblages

Miina Hujala

Miina Hujala is an artist and curator based in Helsinki. She holds an MFA from the Praxis exhibition studies programme at the Academy of Fine Arts, Uniarts, Helsinki, and an MA from Aalto University. She was an exchange student at Hongik University in Seoul in 2009 and an intern at The Vera List Center in New York in 2013. Hujala is currently running Alkovi, a display window art space in Helsinki, together with the artist and curator Arttu Merimaa. In 2016–23 she co-curated (also with Merimaa) *Connecting Points*, a Finnish–Russian exchange programme for HIAP, the Helsinki International Artist Programme. In 2021–24 she was artistic researcher and project manager for the *Reside/Sustain* project, focused on residencies and sustainability.

To participate in a residency is a situation of privilege, founded on the possibility to be hosted and facilitated by someone. The feeling of being given something (an opportunity) is there, and the temporary stay is predicated on the possibility of mobility, on the promise and allure of an alternative viewpoint or site or on exposure to discourse that would otherwise not be accessible. The situation of displacement is seen as an asset.

The more we travel for work, the more we are called upon to provide institutions in other parts of the country and the world with our presence and services, the more we give in to the logic of nomadism, one could say, the more we are made to feel wanted, needed, validated, and relevant.[1]

1 Residencies have been flourishing in the global era. Miwon Kwon notes that mobility has been seen as paramount in the accumulative sense. Miwon Kwon, *One Place After Another: Site-Specific Art and Locational Identity* (Cambridge, MA: MIT Press, 2004), p. 156.

The question of mobility in times of globalisation has been widely and regularly contested. It is – blatantly and obviously – not free, nor always desired and not in any way open for all. The question of how mobilities manifest themselves and are maintained, what is sought after and how (im)mobilities are created is a crucial one, because it connects many elements in the same field.

A very relevant exploration of the topic of mobility is Mimi Sheller's book *Mobility Justice.* It addresses the 'triple crisis' of mobility – climate, urbanisation, refugee – and starts from a 'new mobilities paradigm' according to which mobility is not 'simply a late modern global condition' but has been the 'precondition for the emergence of different kinds of subjects, spaces, and scales'.[2]

Sheller points out that mobilities have histories and that mobilities are always 'contingent, contested, and performative'.[3] *Mobility Justice* enacts a concept for thinking how 'power and inequality inform the governance and control of movement, shaping the patterns of unequal mobility and immobility in the circulation of people, resources, and information'.[4] Sheller ends her book by listing her collated principles for mobility justice.[5]

I would argue that mobility needs to recover from the hangover after a specific need-to-do-more paradigm: the accumulative notion of profit-seeking brought into view as travelling the globe, gaining and using cultural capital and attention, sometimes for very good causes. We therefore need to follow how mobility reintroduces familiar frictions and challenges the practice of art residencies. Residency practice has been about actualising 'positive' globalisation and affirming possibilities for mutual discovery and cross-pollinating exchange.

The idea of travelling as access, built on a beautiful egalitarian vision of the world as home to all, is now hard to believe in, although as beings we still have a mobile existence. The vision of mobility was built on a promise of offering possibilities for exchange and encounters, with the intention to build knowledge of what being-together means. Perhaps also with the intention to explore what it means to inhabit versatile and multiple cultures and to create more complex – but perhaps also more honest and communal – futures together.

THERE ARE DISTANCES AND DURATIONS

2 Mimi Sheller, *Mobility Justice: The Politics of Movement in an Age of Extremes* (New York and London: Verso, 2018), p. 9.

3 Ibid., p. 10.

4 Ibid., p.14.

5 Ibid., pp. 173–4.

6 Based on research by the eco-coordinator Saara Korpela, who calculated the imprint of three Finnish organisations. More information from her seminar documentation: https://www.ihmehelsinki.fi/en/2020/12/eco-seminar-feedback-and-documentations/ (accessed in February 2024).

In 2018 we embarked on our first Trans-Siberian train journey as an artistic research trip organised as part of the Finnish–Russian exchange programme *Connecting Points* within HIAP, the Helsinki International Artist Programme. One of the concerns behind the project was to find alternative ways of travelling to lessen the impact of earth-warming emissions. Since flights are a major contributor to the CO_2 load of any residency organisation, we looked into long-distance train travel.[6] *Connecting Points* was curated by myself and Arttu Merimaa from 2016 until 2020 and by myself until 2023.

The idea behind using the Trans-Siberian route through Russia was based on geographical and infrastructural realities: our ability to reach the Pacific coast (the city of Vladivostok) by train from Helsinki, and the possibility of continuing to China, Japan or South Korea. Our aim was to utilise this route as a part of art residency exchanges, so that residents would be able to travel together to residency stays in Tokyo, Beijing or Seoul (as

7 We started the Trans-Siberian train journeys within the *Connecting Points* programme in 2018 and continued it in 2019 with support from the Finnish Cultural Foundation, which had residency partnerships in the cities mentioned. The project was first postponed due to Covid-19 and then the plans to travel on Trans-Siberian route were terminated in 2022 when Russia started its war against Ukraine. The project continued with a sea-based trip to Iceland in 2023. The *Connecting Points* programme ended the same year.

well as to possible sites in Russia) and also make use of the travel time as a part of the residency.[7]

Before our first trip in 2018 I couldn't fathom how durational travel would feel. By durational I mean staying on board the same vehicle for multiple days. It was more pleasant than I expected and, more importantly, more rewarding than any option that would have privileged speed and directness, which usually means flying. To just sit and do nothing felt like a blessing.

It felt as if time evaporated but also became more tactile. The days dissolved into each other. The rhythm of the stops, the eating, reading and sleeping sessions, the discussions with my fellow travellers: this made me feel that time was just something to come to terms with. The fact that we were constantly in movement also really helped. Spending time can be meaningful or drastically excruciating. We don't have to determine what it will be beforehand but we should be mindful of making assumptions and instead notice the actual changes.

The train project used the Trans-Siberian route almost as a mobile residency where people could spend time together while travelling for a month or so, eastwards and back west. My underlying thesis was that opening up a pre-existing mode of transit as a form for new opportunities would bring forward more than a merger of constituent parts. I was thinking that when people share the time it takes to travel, when they eat and discuss and work together and, perhaps most importantly, when they experience things jointly, then more is gained than mere transition.

I tried to find an allegory for how durational travel felt to me when we made another trip with a small group in 2019 and I explored being on a train all the way from Vladivostok to Moscow, staying in a compartment for almost seven days.[8] It was like being in a cabin in the woods, or on a trek.

But was it a residency? I'm hesitant to give it that name, because it was so much about passing through and exploring, and because the group had been formed as an artistic research team, not as a contingent of residents. I think a residency should include the possibility to be in a place with other people working and living there, but *without any obligation to communicate or collaborate.* Sometimes the setting may be more residential, more akin to neighbourly living, and sometimes more vacational/ vocational, a place to rest and ponder and develop one's skills, or a work-shop/productive-get-togethery where the focus is on doing a specific project or networking.[9]

For me the most crucial thing about residencies is that they are facilitated activities. They are not self-organised but provided. The facilitator, usually an institution, assumes the role of shaping practices and possibilities. What is wanted or sought from the resident is participation, at least in some form, perhaps just being present on-site or within a context. This is reflected in reports for funders and sometimes it is enough. Most of the time the logic of distribution is formed with a gatekeeper's mindset. Who is allowed to enter residencies as sites of attention? Residencies are also sites for career-building and some offer participants a concrete possibility to sustain themselves, in the form of a grant or per diem.

I'm thinking of what it would mean if residencies were to be truly mobile in their practice, contributing to this issue with an institutional awareness of the complexity it entails. From travelling to the static experience of being on-site, from commuting to communicating across distances. To be truly mobile, how should residencies formulate their agenda, secure the resources they depend on or define their points of entry and exit? It is easy to see a residency taking place on a train as mobile in a very concrete sense, but in this instance, what I have in mind is an exploration of mobility that also uproots some parameters linked with residencies as art institutions.

Residencies could challenge the perceived necessity to be recognised as progressive by being accumulative. They are expected to create continuously more attention and connections

8 You are not totally encapsulated on the train even though you stay on board for the entire route. Making overnight stops along the way is of course an interesting part of the journey. In 2019 and 2018 we stepped off the train for multiple overnights stops. Only on the return journey to Moscow in 2019 did we spend all our nights on the train.

9 I want to note that different modes coincide and criss-cross, and that the residency field is in constant movement. There is obviously constant discussion about the kinds of programmes that actually contribute to the definition(s) of what a residency is.

for people, practices and places. This allows residencies, as art institutions, to be perceived as socially present, attuned and informative. Acknowledging these expectations as a pressure to perform accumulation is part and parcel of challenging the often problematic pursuit of value.

ASSEMBLAGES AND ASSOCIATIONS

Some books offer ways of finding common ground and become sources to gather around. I have noticed that Anna Lowenhaupt Tsing's thought-provoking *The Mushroom at the End of the World: On the Possibility of Life in Capitalist Ruins* (2015) is often discussed, and I have taken guidance from it myself as I made my path through residency practices and mobility. Thinking about art residencies, travel, capitalism and accumulation is also about grasping that movements and material practices are not only connected but coinciding, that they constantly and simultaneously enact relation-making. There is no such thing as singular, disconnected, un-embedded being. Whenever we describe things we become constituted as a part of the description. And the description is not without its own agency and materiality.

Lowenhaupt Tsing writes about 'assemblages' as performances of liveability.[10] There are multiple ways of making such assemblages, and the book offers different views and stories from where the matsutake grows, whether in Oregon (USA), Yunnan (south-western China), Lapland (northern Finland) or central Japan. Tracking the matsutake provides Lowenhaupt Tsing with this notion of indeterminate assemblage as a polyphonic gathering of ways of being.

Assemblages are about interplay, impermanence, emergence, coalescence, changing and dissolving – and about observations that aren't bound to concepts as limitations but depicted as the mixture of myths, livelihood practices, archives, scientific reports and experiments.[11] Assemblages invite ways of exploring that are not solidifying but acknowledge 'disturbance'. It is not a bad thing that follows a harmonious state of being, but rather 'disturbances follow other disturbances'.[12] To follow disturbance

10 Anna Lowenhaupt Tsing, The *Mushroom at the End of the World: On the Possibility of Life in Capitalist Ruins* (Princeton University Press, 2015), pp. 157–58. In her notes, Lowenthaupt Tsing mentions that her usage of 'assemblage' corresponds to Gilles Deleuze's notion of agencement and is a similar attempt at opening up the term 'social'.

11 Ibid., pp. 158–59.

12 Ibid., p. 160.

is to be looking at landscape assemblages, opening up discussions and exploring the dynamics. Disturbance as an analytical tool refers to an open-ended range of unsettling phenomena, also about what is bearable and what is too much, which both depend on the point of view.[13]

This is about living not predetermined and result-orientated but embedded within perspectives, as a way of orienteering and as an active component of the landscape assemblage. I look at art residencies as assemblages that might not build anything like a career but disassemble, reassemble and contaminate living and working conditions. Lowenhaupt Tsing writes:

We are contaminated by our encounters; they change who we are as we make way for others. As contamination changes world-making projects, mutual worlds – and new directions – may emerge. Everyone carries a history of contamination; purity is not an option.[14]

A contaminated diversity works across difference. It is not self-contained but polluted by history of encounters, because 'we are mixed up with others before we even begin any new collaboration'.[15] Residencies as sites for contamination are built on the material flows that mobile humans require. They leave traces of themselves (such as art works) – but with the hope to enter a clean room. The culture of residencies lingers on the steps of inclusive and welcoming benevolence. 'Open call' as a practice is a direct way to see this; it is about offering something, opening up possibility for a space and time but with various hidden physical, mental and fiscal thresholds. It is predicated on the assumption that there will be people coming and going with a certain aptitude. Residencies can be seen as temporal landing sites.

Could this be an advantage? Could residencies be 'sites in which to seek allies'?[16] For Lowenhaupt Tsing, sites of 'latent commons' are not exclusively human, and not for everyone. Nor do they institutionalise well, and they won't redeem us. Latent commons can be best described as ubiquitous but rarely noticeable, and when found unlikely to be found again, and I would take the liberty to rephrase Lowenhaupt Tsing and say that they are bubbling, poisoning, collaborative but partial. Latent commons are like finding treasures amongst the trouble.[17] I see mobility in residencies as predicated on such beneficial instability, where

13 Ibid., p. 161.

14 Ibid., p. 27.

15 Ibid., p. 29.

16 Ibid., p. 255.

17 Ibid., p. 255.

the points of directions are not – indeed cannot and need not be – clearly defined. The elusive coming-together is one form of performing the political.

18 See Bruno Latour, *Down to Earth, Politics in the New Climatic Regime* (transl. Catherine Porter) (Cambridge and Medford, MA: Polity Press, 2018).

19 Ibid., p. 93.

20 Ibid., p. 94.

21 Ibid., p. 95.

DWELLING PLACES AND ACCESS RIDERS

We have to be attuned to the act of making definitions. They are testaments of ongoing navigation and correspondence. Bruno Latour proposes making an inventory of things that acknowledge our crucial dependencies, our boundedness to *terra*, the earth, to soil and to the world. These are not contradictory but complimentary. The listing is a way to orient ourselves as 'terrestrial'.[18] One term that Latour uses is 'dwelling place', which is very apt in the context of residencies. Residencies are places to stay in for a moment. Art residencies can provide an allegory of our mobile ephemeral boundedness. They can also provide a site for inquiry of our conditions and properties.

Each of the beings that participate in the composition of a dwelling place has *its own way* of identifying what is local and what is global, and of defining its entanglements with others.[19]

For Latour, finding something politically graspable is to generate alternative descriptions:

How could we act politically without having inventoried, surveyed, measured, centimetre by centimetre, being by being, person by person, the stuff that makes Earth for us?[20]

These dwelling places must be defined by listing what the terrestrial 'needs for its subsistence, and, consequently what it is ready to defend, with its own life if need be'.[21] These are the properties the terrestrial possesses and depends on. If deprived of them, it would disappear.[22] For Latour this inventory, the description of interests, demands and grievances, is 'an experiment worth attempting'[23] as a way to make up a world that would be more or less sharable. It enables us to have an inhabitable ground and to counter the disorientation and loss that people feel whether they perceive themselves as 'natives' or 'foreigners'. All are looking for refuge somewhere. This is a mobile grounded belonging. The political is 'atmospheric'.[24] It evades our grasp but is tacitly present. Politics is the entity's dispersed knowledge of itself.[25]

Making visible requirements and demands is something that becomes manifest in the practice of 'access riders'. The term has been adapted from the practice of merely making additional list of requests or clauses (riders) to agreements and is now used beneficially for attending to crucial and specific needs and securing access for persons with disabilities.[26]

The benefit here is not to see access riders as a form of contract making but as an opening to a correspondence. '[The access rider] can work as a starting point for a conversation between the inviter and invitee about the accessibility of a certain situation.'[27] The access rider is a way to ignite discourse and start collaboration. I see this as a method for disclosing assumptions and dependencies. When done right it becomes a description of our dwelling, understood as the required precondition for participating in the political.

22 This list-making is a challenge, Latour admits, but then goes on to give us an example of the situation of 1789. In the 'ledger of complaints' notes about necessary reforms were gathered, formed as lists of grievances in which where people were able to describe themselves and their dwelling places.

23 Ibid., p. 98.

24 Ibid., p. 93.

25 I have also benefitted from the introduction by Turo-Kimmo Lehtonen to the Finnish translation of the book. Lowenhaupt Tsing also brings up Latour in her notes and stresses that assemblages are sporadic but consequential coordinations and that 'assemblage' doesn't relate to Latour's actor–network theory. Latour mentions Lowenhaupt Tsing's aforementioned book as an important contribution to 'learning to live in capitalist ruins'.

26 For more about Access Riders, see for instance Charlotte Jacob-Maguire's text: https://www.artsmontreal.org/app/uploads/2021/11/access_rider.pdf, (accessed in February 2024).

27 Quoted from Jessie Bullivant and Jemina Lindholm: https://frame-finland.fi/en/resources/access-riders/ (accessed in February 2024).

For art residencies this means listing their dependencies as institutions and understanding their transitory nature, which includes a possibility to discover and make public the things they stand for. Doing it right means making these listings or presentations without defining 'for whom' or 'for what purpose' they are made.

THE HABIT OF SERVICE

The reason I think it is important to remove the definitions of the subjects for whom this kind of agreement is made is that too many such disclosures are made with funders and other similar actors in mind. They serve a purpose, and too directly. 'Access riders' can be tools for communication and manifestation, but we should avoid constantly trying to meet the demand for providing services.

Yes, residencies are crucially about constant exchange and responsive collaboration (with all the contamination this entails), but we have to be wary. Whenever our descriptions become enclosures, what they describe tends to solidify too quickly into something that aims at travelling beyond the present circumstances to further legitimise our practice. This, of course, is often the intention: an ability to be political. But listing things can be merely about demanding, and just another mode of accumulative comparison. When we make descriptions we instead need to poke holes into them constantly, otherwise we start to police and polish our thoughts too quickly, to make ourselves sound reasonable.

Mobile residencies have a capacity for stabilising the ground, concentrate on providing the space and time for artists (and others) to temporarily situate and displace themselves. Residencies think about hospitality and are concerned with filling the needs and requirements of their participants[28], but they do face the threat of becoming mere service providers, because we are all infused with the habits of service culture.[29]

I would prefer it if the mobility element also entailed that residencies, as constellations, should misplace themselves. They are filled with passing encounters. An encounter has to be a radical opening and exposure. This cannot happen if we have preconceived ideas about it; then there is no real encounter.[30]

Residencies should not create (or be) opportunities for artists. Facilitating is different from producing. It means supporting or staging a possibility for things to happen without aiming for any particular result. Yet these expectations are also brought by us who participate in residencies, because the market economy is always present with its funds and availabilities, needs and services. The problem is not that we are full of expectations, but that we expect them to be fulfilled.[31] We are taught to accept the terms of the service economy, and residencies are seen as providers for artistic work. It is hard to open up the power structures of mutual dependency and make alternative mappings and routings.

The need to attune constantly can also be a trap. Adaptivity is seen as a source for finding a role and a place in a situation of change, within a flow of energies, resources and cultural value-production. It can be a source of vitality but also of exploitation. When defining a place to stand and situate oneself in is a

28 With 'participants' I mean the quite versatile roles, acts and directions of meanings that the activity of enabling a residency entails; from residents and funders to the societal, monetary, ecological, 'ego-logical', conceptual and material circuits.

29 One concept in which this is manifested is the idea of nature as an 'ecosystem service provider' for humans. This is obviously very limiting and makes economic and measurable relations the key perspective for understanding and providing the settings for actuality. Ville Lähde, in his book *Niukkuuden maailmassa* ('In a World of Scarcity'), instead uses the term 'environmental commonwealth' (p. 90, translation by the author) to denote elements of quality and perspective beyond human activity. Lähde has nothing against the term 'ecosystem service', since words themselves don't necessarily support the associations they give rise to. I agree, we must commit to the constant translation, calibration, defining and (re)purposing of words and concepts.

30 Summarised from a lecture by Elisabeth A. Povinelli at the event *ARS22 Gathering* at Museum of Contemporary Art Kiasma in Helsinki on 11 October 2022, organised during the exhibition titled 'Living Encounters'.

31 This is obviously a limiting predisposition, catering to our requests and wishes and cutting away the unexpected discoveries of 'contaminated collaboration'.

form of resistance against the fluidity and the constant motion that is required from us, it will be a position of endurance and rest. What matters is how we approach the quest both to solidify and to be open.

Such 'sitedness' doesn't look at how dependencies are evaded but at how they are appreciated and welcomed. It is about in situ co-creation. As Lowenhaupt Tsing remarks, 'Matsutake and pine don't just grow in forests; they make forests.'[32]

DEMAND LANDSCAPE

In a situation where being a responsive and responsible actor is a question of good resource management, due to the strong ties that binds any accountability to economic accountability, it is not possible, nor a realistic aspiration, to place all participants on a balanced and equal footing in some predetermined way. This is also because there are – and should be – different roles, situations and settings. But being a mere service provider hides and hinders many of these. Limiting the diversity leads to stagnation.

This limiting starts with the preconceived need to define the roles of the engagement from a particular angle. If we privilege relationships based on service, we also face the threat of nullifying complexity. We risk sacrificing the 'dirt' of soil and contamination to produce 'clarity' in the form of a *quid pro quo* (something given or received in exchange for something else).

Not all relationships are transactions, and many definitely don't need to follow any logic. The good intentions behind making demands may fall prey to the service setup. Residencies may feel obliged to accommodate demands to alleviate transactional imbalances. They may be seen as permanently sited assets when their residents are embedded in the mobile transitory precariat.

Residencies are material practices that are culturally habituated. They activate and are activated by reasons and purposes. They make alliances and distinctions, and they are places to stay in, to move into and out of. Residencies shouldn't feel blind to the kind of constellations that actually determine what they are. To see residencies as service providers limits roles, practices, connections and relationships. This can turn residents into mere consumers.

Attuning to residents' expectations can be a form of finding common ground. It is valuable, and many residency practitioners are very good at it. But what I object to is when the relationship is fully predicated on always moving along the same trajectory, from someone to someone else, becoming akin to a transaction. Service encompasses many beneficial and rewarding acts. It is a valuable thing to provide and shouldn't be treated as something to discard.

I want to stay away from limiting totalisations. I don't want critical suggestions to be perceived as rules on the lines of 'this should not be done'. While we aim at escaping the limiting aspects of the service economy and its mindset, we should also embark on an exploration of the 'demand landscape'.

In this joint journey it is necessary to look for roles that are more versatile than the poles of provider and recipient. The aspiration for accumulation should not become the shared target and purpose. We should not aspire to giving, having, gaining, receiving, providing, using more space, time, attention, resources or distance. We often speak of the quest for common ground as motivated by wants and needs. This is our cultural habit. But it is another thing also to allow it to be accompanied by an accumulative ethos.

32 Lowenhaupt Tsing, op. cit., p. 152.

33 The paradox of how to provide value characteristics without the need for scalability is to allow the 'not enough multiplicity' to actually open ways of seeing/doing/enabling/acting difference. As impossible terrain for measurement.

34 Lowenhaupt Tsing, op. cit., p. 128.

35 Ibid., p. 133.

SALVAGED FROM ACCUMULATION

We already live amongst, through or with many things, thoughts, practices or materials, so to make accumulation, or the culmination(s) of value, visible is just not enough.[33] One term that Lowenhaupt Tsing uses is 'salvage accumulation', referring to the pursuit of profit in all conditions: the 'creation of capitalist value from non-capitalist value regimes'[34] and, more directly, 'turning worlds into assets'. 'Capitalism in itself is an assemblage, a translation machine for producing capital from all kinds of livelihoods, human and not human.'[35]

I have wanted to think how escape may be incorporated into the logic of the service economy, and encourage to notice our dependencies, one of which is the logic of accumulation. For Lowenhaupt Tsing salvage accumulation is the act of 'taking advantage of the value produced without capitalist

36 Ibid., p. 63.

control'.[36] She compares this to capitalist farms where farmers depend on the digestion of animals or photosynthesis. It is about taking advantage of the capacities of ecosystems, as when capitalism doesn't produce oil but indeed thrives from it.

Lowenhaupt Tsing describes the sites where this salvage is 'pericapitalist': both inside and outside capitalism. Value is translated by supply chains. Bluntly put, supply chains submit things to accumulation, bring them under capitalism. 'Pericapitalist economic forms can be sites for rethinking the unquestioned authority of capitalism in our lives.'[37]

37 Ibid., p. 65.

This, for her, is a question of diversity rather than a uniformity of totalising capitalism that must be overcome.[38] The most important thing is to look at where and how such translations take place, how salvage accumulation happens, how 'the skill of sewing learned at home is brought to the factory to benefit the owners', as in one of Lowenhaupt Tsing's examples. She explores the supply chains of matsutake trading and the translation from gift to commodity and back.

Now I look at how the concept of 'discarded excess' (of the facilitated commodity of time) is at risk of being turned into market value. I suggest that this could become an avenue for 'noticing'[39] and inhabiting living assemblages as ways to find refuge from accumulation. The basic idea is to take time to explore what is here. I return to the mobility of a residency, to the movement that allows one to reside with one's abilities, but also to unsettle, uproot and disturb the supply chain operation.

THRIFTING TO FLEE MARKETS (DRIFTING TO FLEA MARKETS) BECAUSE WANDERING IS WONDERING

Flea markets are tactile examples of material (over)production in search of value. They are salvage accumulation in the making. Finding things in flea markets is not only about navigating through predetermined spots to look for something specific, to fill a specific need. Importantly, flea markets offer the possibility of discovery, of finding and placing value on things and salvaging them from oblivion. For me these random assortments of objects, paired with a cacophony of prices, offer a peep into the merger of treasure and trash that is the cultural condition of capitalism.

The value of things is determined without any referent, without entering the market.

Here the concept of the ruin – infused with romantic nostalgia for a lost past – connects with untimely trash. There are relics from the recent past, such as mobile phone covers from the early 2000s that have just escaped the landfill. They are looking for a translator to enter the scene, to make their material existence commodity once again.

Wandering doesn't have an entry or end point; the route is found along the way. It is hard for capitalism to tap into wandering, since it cannot be controlled (if it is to be truly wandering). The control that capitalism aims for is to tap into these flows and impose its navigation systems. Maps apps showing us the way, discussion forums telling us what a discarded commodity object is worth. But wandering and valuing things cannot be controlled, because the attachment to things (objects, places, sites) whose existence you couldn't imagine is about unruly discovery. Flea markets are a testament to our productive and consumptive ethos infused with nausea and the excitement that comes with making finds.

Residencies (not residents) that are wandering become constellations of contaminated diversity. There are expectations that might not be fulfilled, and that is okay. Like in flea markets, nothing was promised, but everything could be discovered. Mobility is hitch-hiking and making things is residual; residencies are both tourist attractions and warehouses for nascent capacities. They are places for attuning to material (and other) dependencies. Thrifting is thriving. Combatting the need for accumulation is taking time to look at what is there/here.

38 Lowenhaupt Tsing values but questions both the post-capitalist optimism of J. K. Gibson-Graham and the homogeneity of the critics of capitalism such as Hardt and Negri.

39 Lowenhaupt Tsing brings forward the 'wall we have built between concepts and stories' (pp. 158–59). In trying to distill a general principle, science theorists end up draining the significance of sensitivities. Lowenhaupt Tsing proposes an alliance of the arts of ethnography and natural history, committed to observation and fieldwork – what she calls 'noticing'.

From Rihla to Hakawātī: On the Overlooked Histories of Art Residencies

Pau Català

Dr. Pau Catà is an artist, curator and researcher based in Barcelona. In 2009–23 he was the coordinator of CeRCCa and in 2017–23 of Platform Harakat. Since 2020 he is a founding member of ARRC – Art Residency Research Collective. He holds a Doctorate in Art from the University of Edinburgh and is currently teaching at UOC, Catalonia Open University. Dr. Catà's research focuses on alternative histories, nomadology, experimental methodologies and intellectual heritages and has been awarded multiple grants and fellowships. Recent online publications include 'Icarian Journeys' (*Big Sur Series* 2, 2022), 'Mediterranean alternatives: Towards a speculative art residency proto-history' (*IDEES*, 2020), 'Towards the post-Digital in the Humanities? (*Artnodes*, 2018), 'Beyond Qafila Thania: Walking as immediate and preterit empathy' (*Walking Art/Walking Aesthetics*, 2018) and 'Rethinking decolonial dualism' (*Re-visiones*, 2017).

As I write these lines I find myself in an old house in the Catalan countryside. This house, where my mother and her sisters grew up, became an art residency in 2009, after long years of stillness and decay. Its vernacular name, Cal Tinentu, was replaced by the new and rather pompous acronym CeRCCa, the Center for Research and Creativity Casamarles.[1] Since then CeRCCa has functioned as a temporary residency, a living and working space where artists from all around the world have been inspired to develop and share their experiences and knowledge.

This way of being in the world was suddenly interrupted in March 2020, when the pandemic made us confront our vulnerability and acknowledge the limits of our practices as artists, curators and researchers. In this shifting and unpredictable context, a concern arose amongst a certain community of practice that, until then, had accepted the privilege of artistic mobility as a given. How to facilitate the experience of an art residency when one of its core premises, that of humans gathering to experience something unknown, was no longer possible? How to reconnect with one another, with our surroundings and unknown others, from a place of isolation? Where, in such limiting circumstances, did the value of travelling and the journey reside?

Foreshadowing these concerns, the historian Houati Touati states, 'We are living the death of something that is essential: the *voyage*.'[2] For Touati, in our contemporary context 'there are no more travellers; their race has disappeared. All there is left is tourists, those who never take on a destination without turning it into an industrial formula for a sojourn.'[3] What he is referring to is the realisation that 'the "identical" has spread over the planet under the alienating form of the market and the fetishism of merchandising'.[4] Touati is not alone when formulating his preoccupations. In *Residencies and future cosmopolitics* (2017) the Finnish curator Taru Elfving asks to overcome the 'age of innocence'.[5] An age in which international mobility within the creative sector has been uncritically promoted.

To start addressing this situation I want to suggest that one of the steps we might want to consider is to turn our gaze backwards. By investigating the pasts of art residences we will be able to rethink a historiography that is not only limiting but also grounded in facile approaches. These are formulated from at least two assumptions. First, that art residencies originate as a Western phenomenon in the Modern era.[6] Second, that their genealogy is intrinsically linked to the production of artistic objects. Although the current account might for some be satisfactory, this essay wants to stress that its revision can potentially open up more exciting prospects. This paper is an attempt to animate research on the possible pasts of art residencies and their overlooked histories.

The project presented here therefore moves away from both Western-centric approaches and the production of aesthetic objects and focuses instead on the practices of knowledge exchange and journeying within a specific field, namely Arab and Islamic intellectual heritages. This geographical and cultural shift responds not only to the persistent calls to provincialise Europe – famously voiced by Dipesh Chakrabarty in 2000 – but also to both personal and professional circumstances.

1 www.cercca.cat (accessed in February 2024).

2 Houari Touati, *Islam and Travel in the Middle Ages* (University of Chicago Press, 2010), p. 257. It is important to differentiate between 'voyage' and 'journey'. Although the two practices are related to the notion of travel, in the sense of 'going from one particular place to another', journey refers to a singular travel event while voyage is a long journey. In this paper the practice of 'residency hopping' is related to a lifestyle closer to that of the voyager.

3 Ibid.

4 Ibid.

5 Taru Elfving, 'Residencies and future cosmopolitics' (keynote). Available at: https://www.kunsten.be/en/now-in-the-arts/residencies-and-future-cosmopolitics/ (accessed in February 2024).

6 Because of its visibility and influence the historical account most available nowadays is the one provided on the Transartists website. Available at: https://www.transartists.org/residency-history. It goes as follows: 'The first wave of artist-in-residence programmes, as we still know them, arose around 1900. In the United Kingdom and the United States, art-loving benefactors regarded the offering of guest studios to individual artists as a new kind of romantic patronage. In the same period, artists themselves settled in the countryside and collectively tried to realise their artistic ideas.' This narrative is complemented in two other texts, the short essay on the origins and development of artist residencies in the thoughtful *Policy Handbook on Artists' Residencies*, a study commissioned by the European Commission and carried out in 2014 by a working group of experts on artist residencies from EU member states.

Since 2009 I have, as part of my position as coordinator of CeRCCa, intended to establish collaborations with like-minded initiatives in North Africa and the Middle East. The reasons to do so have been twofold. CeRCCa wanted to address the persistent lack of acknowledgement of the historical ties and hybrid heritages that intertwine Europe and the Arab world. Muslim cultures form a crucial part of my own southern European heritage, but one that continues to be neglected. My thinking was that CeRCCa could become a catalyst in promoting artistic exchanges and community interactions between artists from both sides of the Mediterranean. The aim was to help dismantle the multiple stereotypes towards our southern neighbours that still exist.

It was with these objectives in mind that Platform Harakat[7] was created. Named after the Arabic word for movements, Platform Harakat embodies the inherent contradictions of travelling, that movements occur despite and because of a paradox simultaneously promoting, impeding, and forcing mobility. Through collaborative artistic and curatorial research projects, Platform Harakat has wanted to reflect upon different approximations of the journey, the heritage of its traditions and its erasures, setting in motion concepts and practices derived from mobility and its shadows.

As is the case with *On the overlooked histories of art residencies* and the virtual space *An event without its poem is an event that never happened*[8], the ethos of Platform Harakat has been to document forgotten histories and invisible stories while providing a space for critical reflection and action. In this paper I invite the reader to navigate through the project's virtual space and provide a chrono-graphic account representing a selection of several practices that link knowledge exchange and the journey throughout mediaeval Islam as well as in modern Arab and Ottoman history.

Each of these practices – *rihla, siyaha zāwiya, ḥafalāt* and *majālis* – is approached with the help of several narrative voices. Intertwining storytelling and case-studies, the lives of real and semi-fictional characters as well as past and contemporary situations, my paper will offer historiographical insights into the field of art residencies while at the same time disclosing some of its many overlooked histories.

7 https://paucata.cat/ph/ (accessed in February 2024).

8 https://aneventwithoutitspoem.com (accessed in February 2024).

9 Abd-Allah ibn Abbas (619–87) was a cousin of Prophet Mohammed and one of the early Qur'an scholars.

10 *'Ilm* is the Arabic term for knowledge. In the Western world, 'knowledge' means information about something, divine or corporeal, while in Islam, *'ilm* is a term encompassing theory, action and education. It is not confined to the acquisition of information but also embraces socio-political and moral aspects.

THE GREAT FORGETFULNESS: DAMASCUS, 20 MAY 677

Abd-Allah[9] arrives in Damascus from Basra on a clear and sunny day at the end of spring in 677. Although traditionally inhabited by Eastern Orthodox Christians and Monophysites, over the last decades the city has become home to a community of Muslims from Mecca, Medina, and the Syrian desert. They have in turn made the new capital of the Umayyad caliphate an important centre of Islamic, Christian and Aramaic thought. In the different *halaqahs* (study circles) throughout the city, long and intense debates on theology, epistemology and the nature of *'ilm* (knowledge[10]) are being held daily. Sitting in one of the halaqahs with his followers, Abd-Allah proclaims gravely:

A time will come in which every passing year will be more miserable than the one before it.[11]

The atmosphere has become tense. Abd-Allah raises his head, looks at each of the scholars in turn and affirms:

And I am not speaking of a year less fertile than another or of a sovereign worse than another, but of your scholars, your pious men, and your doctors, who will depart, one after the other, and whom you will not be able to replace.[12]

11 Houari Touati, op cit., p. 26.

12 Ibid.

The imminent disappearance of the *'ilm* produces an anxiety that grips the city. For its impending death recalls the irremediable eclipse of knowledge after the departure of the Prophet Mohammed. How to avoid the danger of loss that hovers over the *'ilm*? How to preserve this knowledge from corruption? How to transmit it in its original purity? These are the urgent questions the Islamic men of letters are faced with. In the midst of this confusion, Abd-Allah states:

He who does not memorise the Qur'an, he is like the
ruined house.[13]

13 Ibid.

It is this singular statement that will shape a new tradition in the coming centuries. Indeed, because the entire Muslim Middle Ages succumbed to the ghost of the great forgetfulness, the scholars of the time cultivated a veritable cult of memory. In this widespread mobilisation, the institution of the voyage came to be seen as a shield against forgetfulness, while knowledge of language came to hold utmost importance. The common belief was that the language that remained closest to the revelation was that of the Bedouins. Spoken in remote lands, it hadn't yet been corrupted. The mission to gather the language from the mouth of the Bedouins became an obsession amongst men of letters of the time. The pursuit of that knowledge justified the *rihla*.

Before departing to his permanent retreat in the city of Taif in today's Saudi Arabia, Abd-Allah turns his head and looks upon his beloved city for the last time. Damascus seems busy and lively, unaware of his affliction and of the great forgetfulness he sees approaching.

This story took place at the threshold where Islam comes into existence, the late seventh century in the Christian calendar, a time when art residencies did not yet exist but where spaces articulating the relationship between the search for knowledge and the journey nonetheless flourished. Over the course of the eighth and ninth centuries, the *rihla*, or travelling as a method of acquiring and documenting knowledge, developed around the *halaqahs*, the first study circles constituted in Islamic urban centres.

Such circles brought together several generations of scholars, the *raḥḥālas* whose sole preoccupation was to search out, collect and compare traditions by travelling from one region to another in the Muslim world. Through the *rihla*, the *raḥḥālas*, the globetrotters of the age, embraced the paradigm of exile and return, and also the idea of the voyage as text, the *'ajā'ib*. Linked to both the narratives of exile and return and the *'ajā'ib* literary genre, an alternative way to acquire and transmit knowledge arose.

This was the *wijada*. The root of the word *wijada*, formed by the consonants w, j, and d, is resonant of the Arabic words for discovery and invention. Although they were seen with suspicion by traditional scholars, discovery and invention became central concepts in the idealised descriptions of the Bedouins made by younger Islamic travellers from the urban cultural hotspots. Sooner than expected, though, through the *wijada* the sojourn in the desert metamorphosed from the desired expedition into a lazy and nostalgic gesture that was no longer possible because of the Bedouins themselves. 'Corrupted by mixing with peasants, city dwellers, and non-Arabs, the inhabitants of the desert eventually brought on the irremediable loss of their linguistic paradise.'[14]

Similarly to the *rihla*, the expedition as a method to achieve knowledge is at the core of L'appartement 22 in Rabat, Morocco, and its long term programme *Expeditions*.[15] Initiated in 2000 by the curator Abdellah Karroum, L'appartement 22 responded to one of Karroum's preoccupations, the exhibition, as concept and practice. For him, the concept of the exhibition fundamentally rests on the idea of an outward movement, geared toward encounter and discovery. As Karroum notes, 'The movement from exhibition to expedition is in my mind the path to take to understand the function of art, and its possible autonomy within Maghrabian societies.'[16]

Resonating with the journey of the ninth-century *rahḥālas*, L'appartement 22's first expedition took place in an Amazigh village in the Rif region. The aim of the temporary residency in the Amazigh community was to invite locals and artists to engage in exchange and discussions about life and the meaning of the creative act. 'In Morocco, many art practices abandon materiality. These practices do not really leave any traces or objects.'[17] Similarly, talking about artistic production in Egypt, Jessica Winegar states, 'The work of making art is often less about the physical construction of the art object ... [than it is about] discourse.'[18]

14 Ibid., p. 27.

15 https://www.appartement22.com (accessed in February 2024).

16 Katarzyna Pieprzak, *Imagined Museums: Art and Modernity in Postcolonial Morocco* (Minneapolis: University of Minnesota Press), p. 196.

17 Ibid.

18 Jessica Winegar, *Creative Reckonings: The Politics of Art and Culture in Contemporary Egypt* (Redwood City, Cal: Stanford University Press, 2006), p. 10.

YOU KNOW OF THE HOW. I KNOW OF THE HOW-LESS: BASRA, 8 MARCH 731

It is a sunny day in the city of Basra in today's Iraq, but within, Rabi'a is dark and gloomy.[19] Her poor parents have both died and today she will be sold into slavery. Her despair won't last for long, though. That same night, her master sees a light surrounding her while she is praying. The image leaves the man captivated and in the morning he frees her. From then on, she forges her own path, pushing her body and soul onto the dusty roads of knowledge. Like many others at the turn of the ninth century, she slowly disappeared towards the desert, carrying but a few belongings, to practise the *'ilm al-batin*, the knowledge of that which lies within.

I want to put out the fires of Hell, and burn down
the rewards of Paradise, as they block the way to
God.[20]

In the desert, Rabi'a led a life of humility and poverty, showing that having a personal bond to the divine was something both men and women were capable of striving for. Indeed, in her lifetime she never called a man her master. Rabi'a thus consciously pursued an independent lifestyle as a woman poet, wandering through the desert in solitude. In so doing, she was following a path that many female Sufi mystics had charted before her as a means of ensuring personal salvation.

It is said that Rabi'a's ascetic practices brought her closer to the *Adbal*: the society of hidden saints whose great cosmic powers allegedly allowed them to alter their psychic states and withdraw their bodies from physical laws. The legend suggests that she was even able to perform divine miracles because of the intimacy she achieved with God through introspection. When she was asked how she discovered the secret, she responded:

You know of the how. I know of the how-less.[21]

When Rabi'a died at the age of 80, her only possessions were an old patched dress-like mantle, a pottery jug and a reed mat that doubled as her prayer rug. Some say she was buried near Jerusalem, in the Kidron Valley, and her tomb was a cult destination throughout the Middle Ages.

Even as specialists in philology, poetry and genealogy were taking great pains to learn from remote communities through the practice of *rihla*, at the turn of the ninth century another emerging class of learned men and women in Islam also began to focus on the desert. They were mystics seeking fundamental alterity in solitude. Although they shared an obsession with the journey, Abd-Allah's and Rabi'a's reasons to be constantly on the move differed greatly.

Like the *raḥḥālas* in search of the remote communities and their 'pure' language, the mystics used the *rihla* to get closer to their master thinkers. Unlike the scholars, however, they soon felt the limitations of *rihla*. For them, it tended to lead to only one aspect of knowledge, the *dhahir*, or knowledge as appearance. In contrast to the *raḥḥālas*, 'the mystics considered themselves to be the bearers of a sort of knowledge that reached beyond obvious causes to decipher the hidden, the *batin'*.[22] This is how the *siyaha*, a new form of travel in search of knowledge, emerged.

Although the practice of the *siyaha* may seem to belong to a bygone era, the journey into the desert continues to be of interest in artistic and curatorial practices. With its focus on experiential immersion into the desert through the practice of walking, two examples of the resonances between the *siyaha* and contemporary artistic projects are Project Qafila and Wonder, wander.

19 Rabi'a al-Adawiyya al-Qaysiyya, or simply Rabi'a al Basri (717–801), was a female Muslim Sufi saint, considered by some to be the first true saint in the Sufi tradition. Her reputation exceeds those of many Muslim men in the early days of Sufism.

20 New World Encyclopedia. Available at: https://www.newworldencyclopedia.org/entry/Rabia_Basri (accessed in February 2024).

21 Ibid.

22 Houari Touati, op. cit., p. 159.

Project Qafila is a transdisciplinary research platform structured through a series of practical researches on trans-Saharan trade routes.[23] Through a nomadic residency, each year a group of artists and non-artists walk through the routes used to criss-cross the desert from the eighth century, embodying and investigating caravan heritage from a contemporary perspective.

Moving away from the Maghreb towards the East, Wonder, wander was a walking residency curated by the Jordanian art residency program Spring Sessions in 2018.[24] The project was loosely structured through a collective pilgrimage, starting from the northern tip of Jordan and ending in Sinai desert lands. Spanning a distance of more than 400 kilometres over the course of six weeks, the project engaged with the act of walking over a changing terrain. The aim was to contribute to the participants' individual research and artistic practices while engaging with the transversal themes of journeying, premonition, foresight and pilgrimage.

23 http://projectqafila.weebly.com (accessed in February 2024).

24 http://www.springsessions.org (accessed in February 2024).

PERTURBED BY QUIETISM

At the turn of the first millennium, most mystics and men of letters were wanderers and preached vagabondage. Yet there were also others who, afraid of erring and getting lost, stayed in one place. A fierce debate soon consumed scholarly circles, pitting those who advocated for vagabondage against those who were inclined towards *stabilitas* or 'living firmly in a place'.

Stabilitas soon became one of the cornerstones of Western monasticism. Introduced by the Rule of Saint Benedict in the sixth century, this principle aimed at confronting the practice of itinerant monks which went from one monastery to another bringing discredit to the monastic life. In the following century, those who chose *stabilitas* grew in number and influence. Their rationale was that the mystics who lived in one place in the service of God were superior to those who travelled through the land as pilgrims. The first did so in the interest of God, whereas the second did so in their own interest. And so, those who stayed in one place came to be considered superior to those who journeyed between many.

In this context we see the resurgence of the *zāwiya*, a religious foundation of quasi-monastic nature, also in Muslim lands from early medieaval times. Originally referring to the cell of a Christian monk, in the Islamic context the *zāwiya* came to describe a small mosque, oratory or prayer room. Besides providing lodging for pilgrims, some *zāwiyas* also contained libraries, schools, mosques, workshops and granaries. They often played an important commercial role by protecting trade routes, all the while facilitating spaces for knowledge production and temporary or permanent stay.

From the fourteenth century onwards, the *zāwiyas* linked to each other forming intricate networks in which scholars and mystics mingled and exchanged ideas while at the same time learned from local experts. Often linked to this network of *zāwiyas*, other practices and places arose in which artisan-artists and scholars could find time and space to network, discuss and perform unburdened by institutional constraints. One of them were the *ḥafalāts*. These gatherings provided much needed intellectual frameworks giving the scholars the opportunity to regain and collapse time and space both as individuals and as part of a collective. As such, the *ḥafalāts* should be understood as places of encounter in which knowledge and the journey could engage in a process of continuous exchange and enrichment.

Although the notion of the resident's superiority over the traveller became widely accepted, it is important to note that sedentarism through the spread of the *zāwiya* and of monasteries all over the mediaeval world should not be taken too literally. For many of them, it was a snare, and their immersion in the crowd a cover-up. Under the appearance of simulated presence, they in fact lived in a fundamental solitude that made them just as absent from the world as if they had been nomads.

With their focus on collaborative translation and experiments in publishing, *Qalqalah*[25] in France and *Kayfa ta*[26] in Jordan and Egypt resonate with the function of the *ḥafalāts*. From a more expanded perspective the cultural space Le18 in Marrakech, Morocco, can also be good case study.[27] Founded in 2013, Le18 is an independent creative platform and exhibition space offering proximity with the

25 https://qalqalah.org/en (accessed in February 2024).

26 https://kayfa-ta.com (accessed in February 2024).

27 https://le18marrakech.com (accessed in February 2024).

28 https://www. think-tanger.com (accessed in February 2024).

29 Mihri Hatun, also known as Lady Mihri and Mihri Khatun (1460–1506), was an Ottoman poet. She was the daughter of a *kadi*, an Ottoman judge, and according to sources she spent most of her life in and near Amasya in Anatolia. She was a member of the literary circle of Prince Ahmed, the son of Sultan Bayezid II.

city's traditional way of life and its surroundings. The project aims to bring the inspiring qualities of the medina into closer contact with the various approaches, practices, and reflections of invited artists.

Amongst many other projects two of the programs that resonate with the alternative art residency history proposed here are *Qanat*, a multidisciplinary and collective platform for research and experimentation exploring the politics and poetics of water and the commons in Morocco and beyond, and *Awal*, an artistic, cultural and social initiative designed to safeguard and enhance the unreturned oral histories of the High Atlas, the Middle Atlas and the Southeast regions of Morocco.

Within this overall focus, it is also important to mention *Think Tanger*.[28] Through publications, podcasts, art residencies and walk-scapes, *Think Tanger* has been a laboratory and platform reflecting, researching and making visible the contemporary urban challenges of the city and its peripheries moving away from exoticising colonial narratives.

THE SAPPHO OF THE OTTOMANS: ISTANBUL, 15 OCTOBER 1498

It is a cold autumn day in Amasya, a prosperous city on the Ottoman Black Sea coast, and Mihri is enjoying herself as she partakes in one of the multiple intellectual court gatherings.[29] Such gatherings, known as *majālis*, have become important cultural nodes, bringing intellectuals together to share, create, tell stories, discuss politics and collectively read books. Contrary to what one might think, a *majālis* did not take place only in elegant palaces and salons. It could also be held in coffeehouses, which were multiplying and forming a network across the city.

Mihri finds herself in the middle of a heated conversation with fellow poets and artists. This is a rare occasion to put forward her ideas, as one of the few women who has been granted access to the early-modern Ottoman intellectual milieu. She says:

It is not gender but intelligence that determines the poet's potential![30]

Some of her companions are astonished to hear such a statement. 'Mihri's existence as a woman poet in the overwhelmingly male literary world of the early-modern Ottoman times is a remarkable feat, as she not only claims a space as a woman, but also to be respected as a Muslim.'[31] Indeed, if a woman did not come from a well-off family that could pay for a private tutor, she would have little chance of obtaining an education. Training opportunities for women in public institutions were scarce, if not non-existing.

Mihri's success as a woman poet in fifteenth-century Ottoman artistic circles can be understood in terms of the institutional milieu of Islamic literary aesthetics. Being well-versed in literary and religious texts, Mihri knew how to legitimately stretch the limits of the aesthetic and intellectual traditions beyond a strictly religious framework. Although she benefited significantly from the alternative pedagogical and residential centres provided by the *zawayas*, Mihri nonetheless knew that she needed to travel if she wanted to be part of the creative networks of the court system and find patrons to sustain her practice.

The need to network and perform is what made travelling from *majālis* to *majālis* essential. Indeed, mobility is what allowed scholars and artists to connect with influential artists and patrons and thus to create a network of financial or educational support. Travelling was not easy for everybody, however. It was in fact considered a dangerous activity, as transportation was limited for both men and women and infrastructure was scarce.

Furthermore, women faced a double threat. Much like in Europe, Ottoman public space was essentially male-dominated. Consequently, women who travelled needed to be protected. If a woman circulated freely, she was considered loose, or out of place and therefore available. As private spaces in which gender and class restrictions could be bent or even obliterated, the *majālis* provided safe spaces for women to share their ideas and connect with other intellectuals.

After a long journey, Mihri temporarily settles in the cultural capital of the Ottoman empire, the Sublime Porte, Istanbul. She is sitting in a corner of her master's coffee-house, a place well known by fortune tellers and poets, engaged in a heated

30 Didem Havlioğlu, 'Mihri Hatun: A Women, a Poet, a Beloved'. Available at: https://trinity.duke.edu/videos/mihri-hatun-a-women-a-poet-a-beloved (accessed in February 2024).

31 Ibid.

discussion on the originality of *ḥanīn ilā al-waṭan* (longing for the homeland), a genre which became highly fashionable in the sixteenth-century Istanbul cultural milieu. Mihri can be heard murmuring:

Truly, Mihri, the heavens have put you far from your homeland. But the condition of exile is pleasant to many hearts.[32]

At the turn of the sixteenth century, the *majālis* or literary salons also constituted important spaces for social and intellectual exchange across much of the Islamic world. Derived from the Arabic root j-l-s, and widely used in both Arabic and Ottoman Turkish, *majālis* literally means 'a place where one sits'. Similarly, the word 'residence' derives from the Latin root *sidere*, 'to sit'. A resident is, then, 'one who remains seated'. While usually formed around a core group of people living in the same city, literary salons became an integral part of elite travel providing 'arenas for discussion among scholars on the move. This is how literary salons facilitated the circulation of books and ideas and the establishment of a shared intellectual tradition.'[33]

Over the course of their travels across Ottoman lands, men of letters, mystics and artists joined the *majālis* that were organised by leading local scholars, becoming, in some cases, residential spaces that structured the practice of the journey. In that context, the politics of visiting and hosting through the *majālis* became essential, accommodating the bearers of multiple travelling narratives throughout the Ottoman Empire. Through diverse strategies, the *majālis* became important nodes of connection and intellectual activity from the fifteenth century onwards. Indeed, they became the places from where scholars, traders, diplomats and artists could articulate the links between knowledge and mobility within the expanding Ottoman Empire. They made it possible for individuals and collectives alike to reclaim time and space, often serving as temporary residencies. In contrast to the institutionalised form of the *zawaya*, the *majālis* were informal structures where scholars and artists could network and gather, share and create, away from dogmatic control.

32 Didem Havlioğlu, hosted by Chris Gratien and Emrah Safa Gürkan, 'Women Literati and Ottoman Intellectual Culture', Ottoman History Podcast no. 71, 24 September 2012, http://www.ottomanhistorypodcast.com/2012/09/women-literati-and-ottoman-intellectual.html (accessed in February 2024).

33 See Helen Pfeifer, 'Encounter after the conquest: scholarly gatherings in 16th-century Ottoman Damascus', International Journal of Middle East Studies Vol. 47, no. 2 (May 2015), pp. 219–239.

In regards to the networked nature of the *majālis*, projects such as Jiser[34] and its triangular residencies between Barcelona, Algiers and Tunis, as well as Madrassa[35] and Travelling Narratives[36] are examples of the persistent linkages that, today and in the past, have existed within the Mediterranean region.

Created in 2016, Madrassa was a fluid network of cultural spaces including Atelier de l'Observatoire (Morocco), aria (Algeria), Mass Alexandria (Egypt) and Spring Sessions (Jordan). Its objective was to facilitate spaces where artists, curators and scholars could mingle and exchange ideas while at the same time learn from local experts. Madrassa supported innovative independent curatorial practices, looking beyond dominant dynamics and modes of intellectual and artistic production. It also explored alternative historiographies.

Likewise, Travelling Narratives was the name of a curatorial and research project developed by Le Cube (Morocco) in collaboration with Townhouse Gallery (Egypt), WaraQ Art Foundation (Libya), L'Espace culturel Diadie Tabara Camara (Mauritania) and Les Ateliers Sauvages (Algeria). In a logic that resonates with the *majālis*, the project articulated a network of artistic residential spaces to collectively imagine new social and cultural utopias based on alternative narratives in North Africa and the Middle East.

PENNY UNIVERSITIES

Together with the *majālis*, coffeehouses flourished in early sixteenth-century Cairo. Henry Castela, an European traveller visiting the city in 1600, noted the presence of many crowded taverns where people drank hot black water at all hours of the day. Coffee was a drink he had obviously never seen before. The history of coffee goes as far back as ninth-century Ethiopia and Yemen. However, it wasn't until the beginning of the sixteenth century that consumption of coffee as a drink was popularised in Egypt. The practice was brought to Egypt by Sufi pilgrims, who drank coffee to stay awake at night for their *dhikr* meditation.[37]

34 https://jiser.org (accessed in February 2024).

35 https://www.atelierobservatoire.com (accessed in February 2024).

36 https://lecube-art.com/exposition/travelling-narratives/?lang=en (accessed in February 2024).

37 Literally meaning 'remembrance or reminder', *dhikr* is a form of Islamic meditation in which phrases or prayers are repeatedly chanted in order to remember God. It plays a central role in Sufi Islam. Each Sufi order adopts a specific dhikr, typically accompanied by specific posture, breathing, and movement.

38 Salah Zaimeche, 'The Coffee Route from Yemen to London in the 10th–17th Centuries', *Muslim Heritage*, 11 October 2010, https://muslimheritage.com/coffee-route-yemen-london/ (accessed in February 2024). For an insightful research on coffee houses see also Areej Abou Harb, 'More than a Cup of Coffee: Stories from the Levant's Great Coffeehouses', https://raseef22.net/english/article/1067725-cup-coffee-stories-levants-great-coffee-houses (accessed in February 2024).

In spite of the ulama's resistance to the use of this intoxicating beverage, very soon it spread from Egypt to Syria and then to Anatolia, reaching Istanbul by the mid sixteenth century. 'By bringing together the diverse elements of society – government officials, tradesmen and artists, the pious and the profane – out of their own closed circles and into the common ground of the coffeehouse, coffee mediated the development of a social design to which everyone could contribute his own knowledge and experience. In that respect, the habit that coffee created in the Islamic world may be said to have laid the foundations of a new civil model that was based on socialisation.'[38]

Coffeehouses and coffee culture soon became an integral part of Istanbul's social life. People came there throughout the day to read books, play chess and backgammon and discuss poetry and literature. Indeed, coffee-houses were dubbed 'penny universities', which describes the social view of these premises as centres of knowledge and is a sign that they were frequented by students, scholars, artists and people of talent. The penny referred to the price of a cup of coffee.

New sociabilities emerged in tandem with the coffeehouse, as they connected a network of travellers and their narratives. Eloquent examples of such travellers can be found in the figures of the *meddah* and the *hakawātī*. The *meddah*, or storyteller, was a travelling artist, whose routes generally linked a network of cities. Upon their arrival in a new city, the *meddah* generally headed straight to the coffeehouse, trusting that they would find a place to perform and to be hosted. The *meddah* often also appears under the name *hakawātī*. The word *hakawātī* is a derivative of the Lebanese *hekaya*, story. As such, the term *hakawātī* designates performers who earn their living by fascinating and captivating an audience with their tales. In mediaeval Islamic times, each village had its own *hakawātī*. However, normally storytellers left their homes and travelled around the region recounting their tales.

39 Salah Zaimeche, op. cit.

40 https://www.ate-lierobservatoire.com/musee-collectif (accessed in February 2024).

Far from being a bygone tradition, the *hakawātī* are nowadays experiencing a revival. In 2014 Dima Matta, a university lecturer, writer and performer in Beirut, restarted the trend of storytelling gatherings with her cliff-hanger storytelling events. Matta's stories typically blend her father's tales of the Lebanese Civil War and her own memories of the time, in which Beirut's power cuts are a recurrent motif. She has stated that she sees the new storytelling events not only as a prolongation of the Middle Eastern *hakawātī* folklore, but also as a way of documenting personal histories that would otherwise go untold.[39] Resonating with storytelling and communal gathering it could be said that the project *Musée Collectif* by L'Atelier de l'Observatoire in Casablanca, also brings together diverse elements of society into a common ground.[40]

BURNING THE BORDERS AND THE SEA

In this alternative art residency history the *harraga* is a fundamental practice that adds further complexity to the relationship between the search for knowledge and the journey within and beyond Arab and Islamic cultures. As in the case of the several models previously proposed, the *harraga* can also become relevant to speculate on several of the complications affecting the field of contemporary art residencies. The tolerance and hospitality experienced by several of the characters in this story is nowhere to be seen in the experience of those that, at the turn of the twenty-first century, and due to economical, political or cultural hardships, have no other option than escaping to other lands. The Algerian Arabic word *harraga* – the action of burning the borders and the sea – designates those who 'burn' their passports and try to seek fortune on the other side of the Mediterranean.

A key characteristic of the socio-political landscape of the twentieth and twenty-first centuries in the Euro-Mediterranean region has been the redefinition of nation-states in neocolonial and identity terms, and a return to the idea of physical frontier as a condition for the restoration of national identity. The design of these new borders does not aim only to safeguard nationalism, but to impose necro-political measures through the application of murdering techniques.[41]

The Schengen Agreement of 1985 was a crucial event in the decision to build up an European identity. The immunised community within the Schengen area rests on a paradox. The fictionalisation of an European identity that is open to free mobility for the same, but puts up borders to protect itself from an invented other. Closely related to both the phenomenon of migration – currently considered illegal as a result of the creation of Fortress Europe – and its touristic exploitation, the Mediterranean continues to be a liminal space crisscrossed by the hopes and speculations of thousands.

Despite sharing the practice of travel, they confront opposite realities. In contemporary societies, the practice of travel has become polarised. Some travel by choice, others are forced to leave their homes and families. The former is expected and received with all kinds of attention and comfort. For the latter, the journey is illegal and, if they reach the destination, they are treated with hostility and forced to confront a reality marked by indifference or xenophobia. This polarisation has profound cultural and psychological consequences. These are what the sociologist Zygmunt Bauman calls the experiences of the 'tourist' and the 'vagabond'.[42] In the current context the disparity between these two travelling experiences takes a dramatic turn which, despite our beloved blindness, is continuously manifested.

41 In 2023, 3041 people died trying to cross the Mediterranean. See https://www.msf.org/mediterranean-migration-depth?gclid=CjwKCAiAnfjy-BRBxEiwA-EECLM9xc-9m7P88-qywEa4yYm-w3NCBvSvpnMj-8feUN4iIMV9TluNbH-gOVxoCtSkQAvD_BwE (accessed in February 2024).

One of the many initiatives confronting EU's border policies and comforting those who live in exile is Hammam Radio.[43] It was created in Berlin in 2020 and can be understood as part of a pattern shaped by the forced mobility of multiple Arab artists and intellectuals escaping the many hardships affecting their homelands. Breaking the boundaries of time and space, Hammam Radio has become a place where women in all their diversity meet, talk, think, and raise their voices. Any woman is free to book a time slot and curate it at will, turning the project into a safe space for all kinds of Arabic-speaking artists in exile.

CONCLUSION: THE ENDLESS JOURNEY

Through an understanding of knowledge production as a fragile and fragmentary endeavour, the excerpts of *An event without its poem is an event that never happened* presented in this essay are examples of how an alternative way to narrate the history of art residencies can be envisioned through artistic and cross-cultural research. Besides the interest in demonstrating the possibility of narrating the history of art residencies otherwise, in this essay I have also tried to stress how the innovative formats art residencies have been adopting since the turn of the twenty-first century may not be as novel as we think.

Ultimately, what *On the overlooked histories of art residencies and An event without its poem is an event that never happened* propose is to engage with a shared history of alterity, which is also a genealogy of communality, to celebrate the ability to live, work, and think otherwise. While I'm advocating for the articulation of art residencies' unforeseen histories, the primary aim of this journey is to discover unexpected lineages, to reside in the movement of knowledge and to rethink the assumptions embedded in a history that we believed was already written.

This essay is based on the research carried out as part of my practice-based PhD in Contemporary Art at the University of Edinburgh in 2016–21, funded by SGSAH, the Scottish Graduate School for Arts and Humanities, and ECA, the Edinburgh College of Art, and awarded the Darat al Funun Dissertation Fellowship for Modern and Contemporary Arab Art in Amman, Jordan. To expand the content of this essay the reader is invited to navigate through *An event without its poem is an event that never happened*, the virtual space created in collaboration with the Marrakech-based curatorial and design duo Untitled as part of the PhD. Through a speculative and creative lens, the virtual space and this text unfold one of the many overlooked histories of art residencies.

42 See Zygmunt Bauman, *Globalisation: The Human Consequences* (New York: Columbia University Press, 1998).

43 https://hammamradio.com/ (accessed in February 2024).

Sources

RESIDENCIES

REFLECTED

SOURCES

Francesca Bertolotti-Bailey: Post-Utopian Communes and Sustainability Camps: Artist Residencies as Machines for Co-Living

Blauvelt, Andrew, *Hippie Modernism*. Minneapolis: Walker Art Center, 2015.
Butler, Judith, *Notes Towards a Performative Theory of the Assembly*. Cambridge, MA: Harvard University Press, 2015.
Chakrabarty, Dipesh, *The Climate of History in a Planetary Age*. University of Chicago Press, 2021.
Dailey, Yvonne, *Going Up The Country: When The Hippies, Dreamers, Freaks, and Radicals Moved To Vermont*. Lebanon: University Press of New England, 2018.
Dall'O, Giuliano and Annalisa Galante, *Abitare sostenibile. Una rivoluzione nel nostro modo di vivere*. Bologna: Il Mulino, 2010.
Davidian, Anne and Laurent Jeanpierre, *What Makes An Assembly? Stories, Experiments and Inquiries*. Antwerp: Evens Foundation and London: Sternberg Press, 2023.
DeLanda, Manuel, *A New Philosophy of Society: Assemblage Theory and Social Complexity*. London: Continuum, 2006.
DeLanda, Manuel, *Assemblage Theory*. Edinburgh University Press, 2016.
Deleuze, Gilles and Félix Guattari, *A Thousand Plateaus: Capitalism and Schizophrenia*. Minneapolis: University of Minnesota Press, 1987.
Deleuze, Gilles and Claire Parnet, *Dialogues II*. New York: Columbia University Press, 1987.
Demos, T.J., *Decolonizing Nature: Contemporary Art and the Politics of Ecology*. Berlin: Sternberg, 2016.
Dmitrieva, Marina and Laima Laučkaitė, *Community and Utopia: Artists' Colonies in Eastern Europe from the Fin-de-Siècle to Socialist Period*. Vilnius: Lithuanian Culture Research Institute, 2017.
Dockx, Nick and Pascal Gielen (eds), *Commonism: A New Aesthetics of the Real*. Amsterdam: Valiz, 2018.
Elfving, Taru, Pascal Gielen and Irmeli Kokko (eds), *Contemporary Artist Residencies: Reclaiming Time and Space*. Amsterdam: Valiz, 2019.
Ghodsee, Kristen, *Everyday Utopia: What 2,000 Years of Wild Experiments Can Teach Us About the Good Life*. New York: Simon & Schuster, 2023.
Hamilakis, Yannis, 'Sensorial Assemblages: Affect, Memory and Temporality in Assemblage Thinking', *Cambridge Archaeological Journal*, 27(1) (2017), pp. *169–82*.
Hampel, Winston and Jack Self (eds.), *Kommunen: Utopian Communes in the New World 1740–1972*. London: Real Foundation, 2020.
Järvensivu, Paavo, 'A Post-fossil Fuel Transition Experiment: Exploring Cultural Dimensions from a Practice-theoretical Perspective', *Journal of Cleaner Production*, 169, no. 15 (2017), pp. 143–51.
Kirksey, Eben, *Emergent Ecologies*. Durham: Duke University Press, 2015.
Kolb, D.A., *Experiential Learning: Experience as the Source of Learning and Development*. Englewood Cliffs, NJ: Prentice Hall, 1984.
Kwon, Miwon, *One Place After Another: Site-Specific Art and Locational Identity*. Cambridge, MA: MIT Press, 2002.
Le Corbusier, *Towards a New Architecture*. London: John Rodker, 1927.
Lübbren, Nina, *Rural Artists' Colonies in Europe 1870–1910*. Manchester University Press, 2001.
Mazzucato, Mariana, *The Value of Everything*. London: Penguin, 2017.
Ndiritu, Grace, *Being Together: A Manual for Living*. Hasselt: KRIEG?, 2021.
Nurmenniemi, Jenni and Tracey Warr (eds), *The Midden*. Helsinki: Garret Publications, 2018.
Pickerill, Jenny, 'Building the commons in eco-communities', Brigstocke, Julian, Leila Dawney and Samual Kirwan (eds), *Space, Power and the Commons*. London: Routledge, 2015.
Ptak, Anna (ed.), *Re-tooling Residencies: A Closer Look at the Mobility of Art Professionals*. Warsaw: A-I-R Laboratory at Centre for Contemporary Art Ujazdowski Castle, 2011.
Puig de la Bellacasa, María, *Matters of Care*. Minneapolis: University of Minnesota Press, 2017.
Richards, William, *Together by Design: The Art and Architecture of Communal Living*. New York: Princeton Architectural Press, 2022.
Sarkis, Hashim (ed.), *How Will We Live Together?, 17th International Architecture Exhibition*. Venice: La Biennale di Venezia, 2021.
Spade, Dean, *Mutual Aid: Building Solidarity During This Crisis (and the Next)*. London: Verso, 2020)
Squatting Europe Kollective, *The Squatters Movement in Europe: Everyday Commons and Autonomy as Alternative to Capitalism*. London: Pluto Press, 2014.

Staid, Andrea, *La casa vivente*. Turin: Add Editore, 2021.

Vargas de Freitas Matias, Rita, *International Artists-in-Residence 1990–2010: Mobility, Technology and Identity in Everyday Art Practices*. University of Jyväskylä, 2016.

Yusoff, Kathryn, *A Billion Black Anthropocenes or None*. Minneapolis: University of Minnesota Press, 2019.

Wiesand, Andreas (ed.), *Mobility Matters Programmes and Schemes to Support the Mobility of Artists and Cultural Professionals*, Study for the European Commission. Bonn: ERICarts Institute, 2008.

Wilk, Elvia, *Oval*. New York: Soft Skull Press, 2019.

Miriam La Rosa: What Next? Art Residences, Time Travelling and Ostension

Barthes, Roland, *Mythologies*. Paris: Editions du Seuil, 1957.

Benjamin, Walter, *The Work of Art in the Age of Mechanical Reproduction* (transl. Harry Zohn). London: Penguin, 2008 [1935].

Berger, John, *Ways of Seeing*. London and New York: British Broadcasting Corporation and Penguin Books, 2008.

Campbell, Enid, 'Ostensible Authority in Public Law', *Federal Law Review* 27, no. 1 (1999).

Carroll, Mark, '"It Is": Reflections on the Role of Music in Sartre's *La Nausée*', *Music & Letters* 87, no. 3 (08/01/2006), pp. 398–407.

Catà, Pau, 'Moving Knowledges: Towards a Speculative Arab Art Residency Proto-History', Edinburgh College of Art, 2021.

Derrida, Jacques, *Archive Fever: A Freudian Impression*. University of Chicago Press, 1996.

Dunkin-Hubby, Laura, 'A Brief History of Mail Art's Engagement with Craft (c. 1950–2014)', *Journal of Modern Craft* 9, no. 1 (03//2016), pp. 35–54.

Eco, Umberto, *A Theory of Semiotics*. Bloomington: Indiana University Press, 1976.

Elfving, Taru, Pascal Gielen and Irmeli Kokko (eds), *Contemporary Artist Residencies: Reclaiming Time and Space*. Amsterdam: Valiz, 2019.

Fesq, Harriet, 'Wupun/Warrgadi: Ngan'gi Fibre and the Art of Peppimenarti', University of Sydney, 2013.

Harris, Gareth, 'Censored? Shadowbanned? Deleted? Here Is a Guide for Artists on Social Media', *The Art Newspaper*, 2021.

La Rosa, Miriam, 'Guests, Hosts, Ghosts: Art Residencies and Cross-Cultural Exchange', The University of Melbourne, 2023.

La Rosa, Miriam, 'Introduction', in Amorim, Margarida B., Alejandro Ball, Miriam La Rosa and Stefania Sorrentino (eds), *In Transition: The Artistic and Curatorial Residency*. London: CtC Press, 2015, pp. 4–11.

La Rosa, Miriam, 'New Start: The Marrgu Residency Program and the Future of Showing', *OBOE Journal* 2, no. 1 (2021), pp. 55–70.

McDowell, John H., 'Beyond Iconicity: Ostension in Kamsá Mythic Narrative', *Journal of the Folklore Institute* 19, no. 2/3 (05/01/1982), pp. 119–39.

McLean, Ian, *Rattling Spears: A History of Indigenous Australian Art*. London: Reaktion Books, 2016.

McLuhan, Marshall, *Understanding Media: The Extensions of Man*. New York: McGraw Hill, 1964.

Michelkevičius, Vytautas, *Mapping Artistic Research: Towards a Diagrammatic Knowing*. Vilnius Academy of Arts Press, 2018.

Noble Wilford, John, '"Venus" Figurines from Ice Age Rediscovered in an Antique Shop', *The New York Times*, 1 February 1994.

Orly, Nanette, 'How Artists Turned to the Postal Service', *Art Guide Australia*, 2020.

Richard, Nelly, *The Insubordination of Signs: Political Change, Cultural Transformation, and Poetics of the Crisis*. Durham, NC: Duke University Press, 2004.

Segal, David, 'An Artist Unites North and South Korea, Stitch by Stitch', *The New York Times*, 26 July 2018.

Shaw, Garry, 'Voluptuous Venus Figurines May Have Helped Prehistoric Europeans Survive the Ice Age', *The Art Newspaper*, 3 December 2020.

Soffer, Olga, James M. Adovasio, and David C. Hyland, 'The "Venus" Figurines: Textiles, Basketry, Gender, and Status in the Upper Paleolithic', *Current Anthropology* 41, no. 4 (2000), pp. 511–37.

Wittgenstein, Ludwig, *Tractatus Logico-Philosophicus*. London: Keagan Paul, 2014 [1922].

SOURCES

Wittgenstein, Ludwig, and G. E. M. Anscombe, *Philosophical Investigations*. London: Blackwell, 1963.

Maria Hirvi-Ijäs: Inertia, Duration, and the Significance of Oblivion: Artist Residencies as Agents of Cultural Sustainability

Cummings, Milton C., *Cultural Diplomacy and the United States Government: A Survey. Cultural Diplomacy Research Series*. Washington: Americans for the Arts, 2009.
Deleuze, Gilles and Félix Guattari, *A Thousand Plateaus: Capitalism & Schizophrenia* (transl. Brian Massumi). Minneapolis: University of Minnesota Press, 1987.
Elfving, Taru, Pascal Gielen and Irmeli Kokko (eds), *Contemporary Artist Residencies: Reclaiming Time and Space*. Amsterdam: Valiz, 2019.
Heinämaa, Riitta, *Suomalainen residenssitoiminta tänään – nykytilanne ja kehittämistarpeet*. Helsinki: Föreningen Konstsamfundet, 2020.
Hirvi-Ijäs, Maria, Sakarias Sokka, Kaija Rensujeff and Ari Kurlin, *Taiteen ja kulttuurin barometri 2018. Taiteilijoiden ja taiteen liikkuvuus*. Helsinki: Cupore Centre for Cultural Policy Research, 2019 (Cupore web publications no. 51).
Holden, John, *Influence and Attraction Culture and the Race for Soft Power in the 21st Century*. London: British Council, 2015.
Huttunen, Mia, *Paha propaganda, hyvä kulttuuridiplomatia?* Helsinki: Tutkijaliitto and the T*iede & Edistys* journal's blog, 5 September 2019.
Ien Ang, Yudhishthir Raj Isar and Phillip Mar, 'Cultural diplomacy: beyond the national interest?', *International Journal of Cultural Policy*, 21:4 (2015), pp. 365–81.
Kokko, Irmeli, Kesä-Kaivo 2021: *My Journey, Research and Exchange*. Helsinki: Kone Foundation, 2021. https://koneensaatio.fi/tarinat-ja-julkaisut/kesa-kaivo-2021-my-journey-research-and-exchange/ (accessed in February 2024).
Kokko-Viika, Irmeli, *Taiteilijaresidenssitoiminnan rooli nykytaiteen tuotannossa*. University of Jyväskylä, 2008.
Muukkonen, Marita, 'Utifrån Ukrainakriget: Nya förutsättningar och utgångspunkter för samarbete med omvärlden', presentation at *Kultur i Almedalen*, Visby, Sweden, on 3 July 2022.
Sennett, Richard, *The Craftsman*. New Haven: Yale University Press, 2008.
Sokka, Sakarias, Vappu Renko and Emmi Lahtinen, *Toimialojen edistäjät ja toiveiden tynnyrit. Taiteen tiedotuskeskusten toiminta ja asema*. Helsinki: Cupore Centre for Cultural Policy Research, 2020 (Cupore web publications no. 60).
Suomi-Chande, Riitta, *Perusteita ja lukuja residenssitoiminnasta. Vinkkejä ja tukea toiminnan aloittamiseen ja ylläpitoon*. Helsinki: Studio Foundation of the Artists' Association of Finland, 2021.
Valtioneuvosto, *Ministeriöiden tulevaisuuskatsaus 2022. Yhteiskunnan tila ja päätöksiä vaativat kysymykset*. Finnish Government and Prime Minister's Office Publication Series 2022:58.
Vargas de Freitas, Rita, *International artists-in-residence 1990–2010: Mobility, technology and identity in everyday art practices*. University of Jyväskylä, 2016.
Weigel, Sigrid, *Transnational foreign cultural policy – Beyond national culture: prerequisites and perspectives for the intersection of domestic and foreign policy*. Stuttgart: ifa (Institut für Auslandsbeziehungen), 2019.

Artinres
https://artinres.fi/category/en/

Artists at Risk
https://artistsatrisk.org/?lang=en

Arts Promotion Centre Finland Taike
https://www.taike.fi/en

Finnish Ministry of Education and Culture
https://okm.fi/en/eu-and-international-cooperation-culture
https://okm.fi/en/creative-economy
https://okm.fi/en/cultural-exports

National Emergency Supply Agency
https://www.huoltovarmuuskeskus.fi/en

Res Artis
https://resartis.org/membership/

Uniarts Helsinki
https://www.uniarts.fi/en/projects/international-incubators-in-fine-arts/

Transartist
https://www.transartists.org/en/about-dutchculture-transartists

Taru Elfving: Residency as Field Work

DeLoughrey, Elizabeth, *Allegories of the Anthropocene*. Durham, NC: Duke University Press, 2019.
Ghosh, Amitav, *The Nutmeg's Curse: Parables for a Planet in Crisis*. University of Chicago Press, 2021.
Hamm, Kalle, *Uusi Pangaia: Kasvimatkoja Seilin saarelle*. Helsinki: CAA, 2023.
Kimmerer, Robin Wall, *Braiding Sweetgrass: Indigenous Wisdom, Scientific Knowledge and the Teachings of Plants*. Minneapolis: University of Minnesota Press, 2013.
Oakes, Selina, 'Post-Residency Interview with artist Kalle Hamm', https://contemporaryart-archipelago.org/publication/post-residency-interview-with-artist-kalle-hamm/ (accessed in February 2024).
Stengers, Isabelle, 'Introductory Notes on an Ecology of Practices', *Cultural Studies Review* 11(1) (2005), pp. 183–96.
Suominen, Saskia, 'Interview with artist Saara Ekström', https://contemporaryartarchipelago.org/publication/interview-with-artist-saara-ekstrom/ (accessed in February 2024).

Vytautas Michelkevičius: Education = Residation? Art Schools as Residencies and Safe Spaces for Artists

Michelkevičius, Vytautas, 'Fairy Tale of a Young Artist, or How to Train Yourself from an Academy Rabbit to a Residency Hopper', Mendrek, Pawel, Elke aus dem Moore, Ika Sienkiewicz-Nowacka, Bojana Panevska, Denise Helene Sumi and Ewa Zasada (eds), On Care: *A Journey into the Relational Nature of Artists' Residencies*. Vienna: Verlag für moderne Kunst, 2023, pp. 207–211.
Müller, Martin, 'In Search of the Global East: Thinking between North and South', *Geopolitics*, 25:3 (2020), pp. 734–55.

Miina Hujala: Bypassing Accumulation: Residencies as Mobile Assemblages

Kwon, Miwon, *One Place After Another: Site-Specific Art and Locational Identity*. Cambridge, MA: MIT Press, 2004.
Latour, Bruno, *Down to Earth, Politics in the New Climatic Regime* (transl. Catherine Porter). Cambridge and Medford, MA: Polity Press, 2018.
Lowenhaupt Tsing, Anna, *The Mushroom at the End of the World: On the Possibility of Life in Capitalist Ruins*. Princeton University Press, 2015.
Lähde, Ville, *Niukkuuden maailmassa*. Tampere: Niin & näin, 2013.
Sheller, Mimi, *Mobility Justice: The Politics of Movement in an Age of Extremes*. New York and London: Verso, 2018.

Pau Catà: From Rihla to Hakawātī: On the Overlooked Histories of Art Residencies

Abou Harb, Areej, 'Stories from the Levant's Great Coffeehouses', *Raseef22*, 14 October 2016. Available at: https://raseef22.net/english/article/1067725-cup-coffee-stories-levants-great-coffeehouses (accessed in February 2024).

Bauman, Zygmunt, *Globalisation: The Human Consequences*. New York: Columbia University Press, 1998.

Elfving, Taru, Pascal Gielen and Irmeli Kokko (eds), *Contemporary Artist Residencies: Reclaiming Time and Space*. Amsterdam: Valiz, 2019.

Elfving, Taru, 'Residencies and future cosmopolitics' (keynote), Flemish Art Institute, 26 May 2020. Available at: https://www.kunsten.be/en/now-in-the-arts/residencies-and-future-cosmopolitics/ (accessed in February 2024).

Havlioğlu, Didem, hosted by Chris Gratien and Emrah Safa Gürkan, 'Women Literati and Ottoman Intellectual Culture', *Ottoman History Podcast* no. 71, 24 September 2012. Available at: http://www.ottomanhistorypodcast.com/2012/09/women-literati-and-ottoman-intellectual.html (accessed in February 2024).

Havlioğlu, Didem, *Mihri Hatun: A Women, A Poet, A Beloved*. Available at: https://www.jstor.org/stable/j.ctt1pk863x (accessed in February 2024).

Open Method of Coordination Group on Artists' Residencies, 'Artists' Residencies: A Short Essay on Their Origins and Development', *Policy Handbook on Artists' Residencies*. Brussels: European Commission, 2014, pp. 69–70.

Pieprzak, Katarzyna, *Imagined Museums: Art and Modernity in Postcolonial Morocco*. Minneapolis: University of Minnesota Press, 2010.

Pfeifer, Helen, 'Encounter after the conquest: scholarly gatherings in 16th-century Ottoman Damascus', *International Journal of Middle East Studies* Vol. 47, no. 2 (May 2015), pp. 219–239.

Touati, Houari, *Islam and Travel in the Middle Ages*. University of Chicago Press, 2010.

Verwoert, *Jan, Exhaustion & Exuberance* (pamphlet for the exhibition 'Yes, No and Other Options'). New York: Dexter Sinister, Sheffield: Sheffield 08 and Geneva: Centre d'Art Contemporain, 2008.

Winegar, Jessica, *Creative Reckonings: The Politics of Art and Culture in Contemporary Egypt*. Redwood City, Cal: Stanford University Press, 2006.

Zaimeche, Salah, 'The Coffee Route from Yemen to London in the 10th–17th Centuries', Muslim Heritage, 11 October 2010. Available at: https://muslimheritage.com/coffee-route-yemen-london/ (accessed in February 2024).

www.aneventwithoutitspoem.com

https://paucata.cat/cercca/

https://paucata.cat/ph/

www.transartists.org/en

www.msf.org

www.appartement22.com/

www.projectqafila.weebly.com/

www.springsessions.org/

www.qalqalah.org/en

www.kayfa-ta.com/

www.le18marrakech.com/en/home/

www.jiser.org/

www.atelierobservatoire.com/

www.lecube-art.com/exposition/travelling-narratives/?lang=en

www.think-tanger.com/

183